FOR ORGANS, PIANOS & ELECTRONIC KEYBOARDS

E-Z PLAY TODAY

196

THE BEST OF
George Gershwin
2ND EDITION

Cover photo: © Photofest

GERSHWIN and GEORGE GERSHWIN are registered trademarks of Gershwin Enterprises
IRA GERSHWIN is a trademark of Gershwin Enterprises
PORGY AND BESS is a registered trademark of Porgy and Bess Enterprises

ISBN 978-1-4584-5960-2

HAL•LEONARD
CORPORATION

7777 W. Bluemound Rd. P.O. Box 13819 Milwaukee, WI 53213

In Australia Contact:
Hal Leonard Australia Pty. Ltd.
4 Lentara Court
Cheltenham, Victoria, 3192 Australia
Email: ausadmin@halleonard.com.au

Visit Hal Leonard Online at
www.halleonard.com

Bess, You Is My Woman

from PORGY AND BESS®

Registration 3
Rhythm: Fox Trot or Ballad

Music and Lyrics by George Gershwin,
Du Bose and Dorothy Heyward
and Ira Gershwin

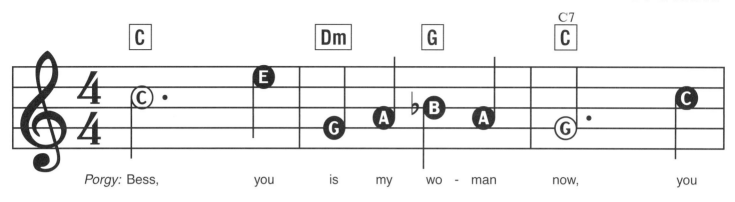

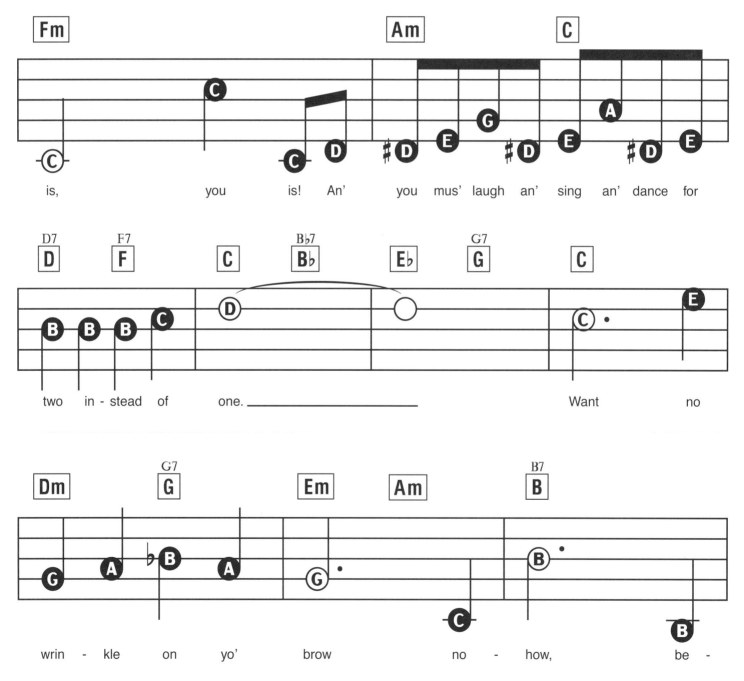

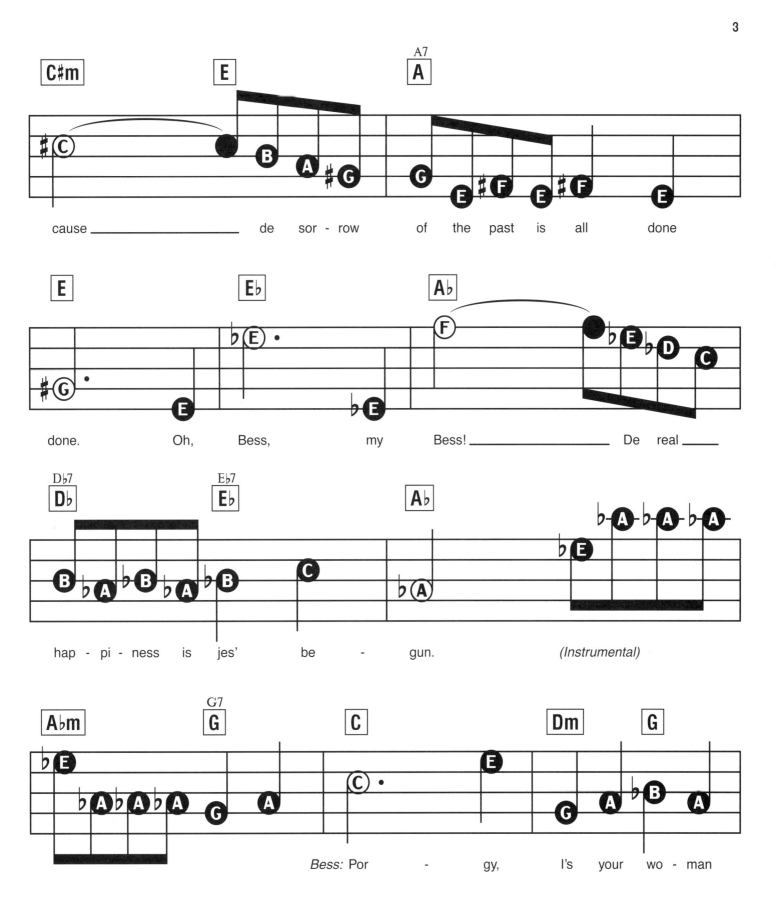

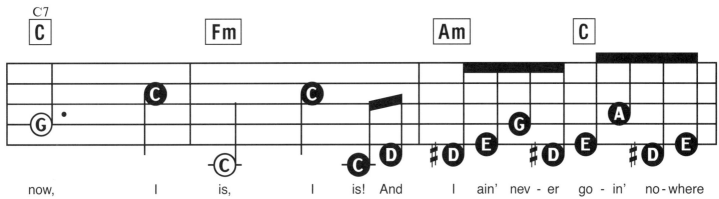

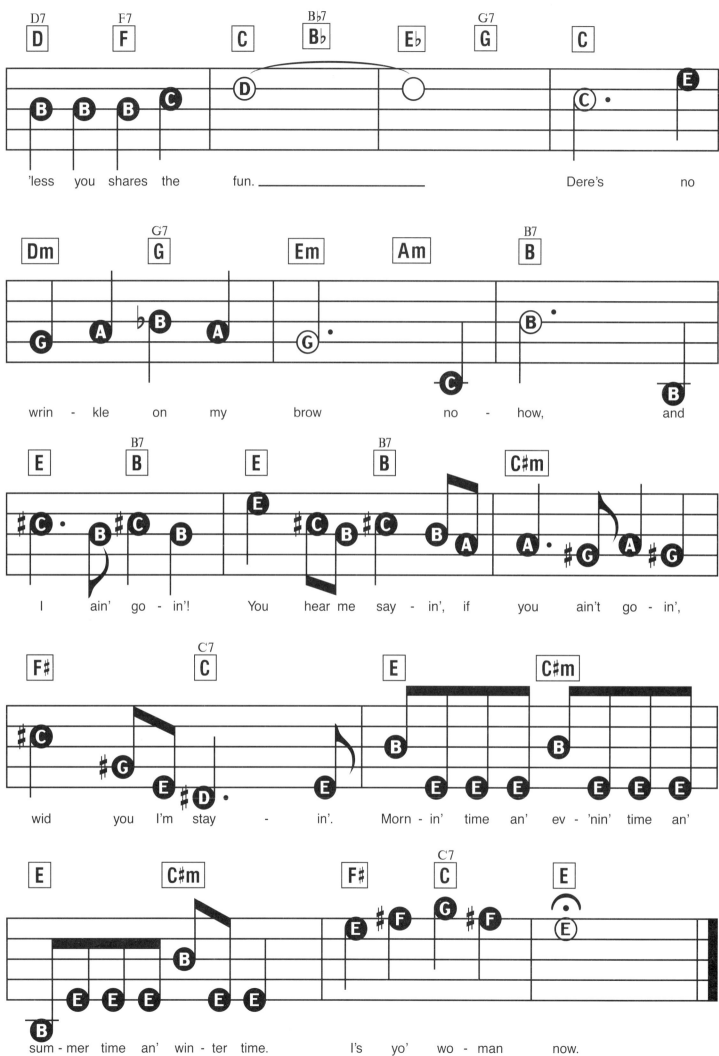

I Got Plenty o' Nuttin'

from PORGY AND BESS

Registration 7
Rhythm: Fox Trot or Country Western

Music and Lyrics by George Gershwin,
DuBose and Dorothy Heyward
and Ira Gershwin

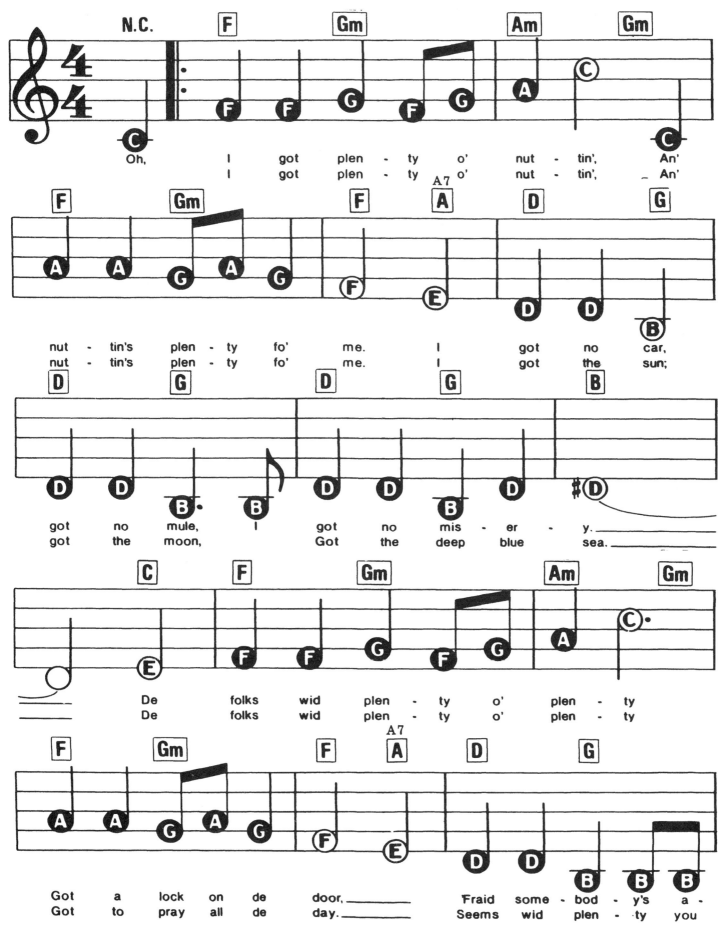

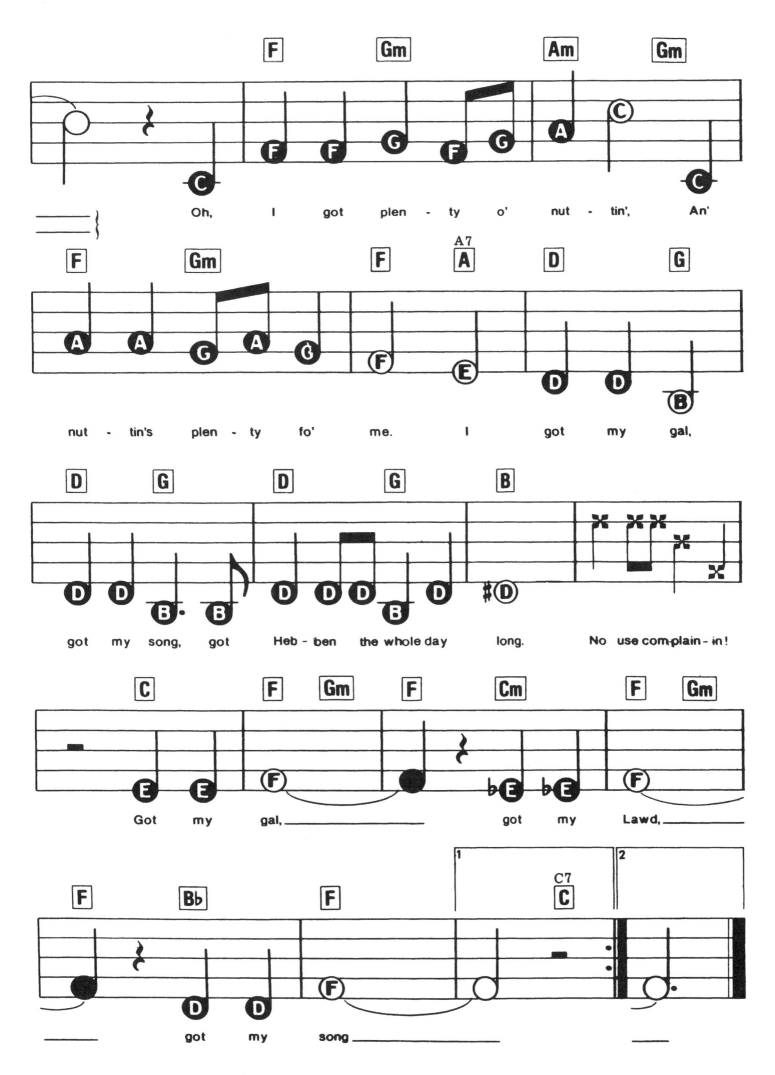

Bidin' My Time

Registration 3
Rhythm: Fox Trot or Swing

Music and Lyrics by George Gershwin
and Ira Gershwin

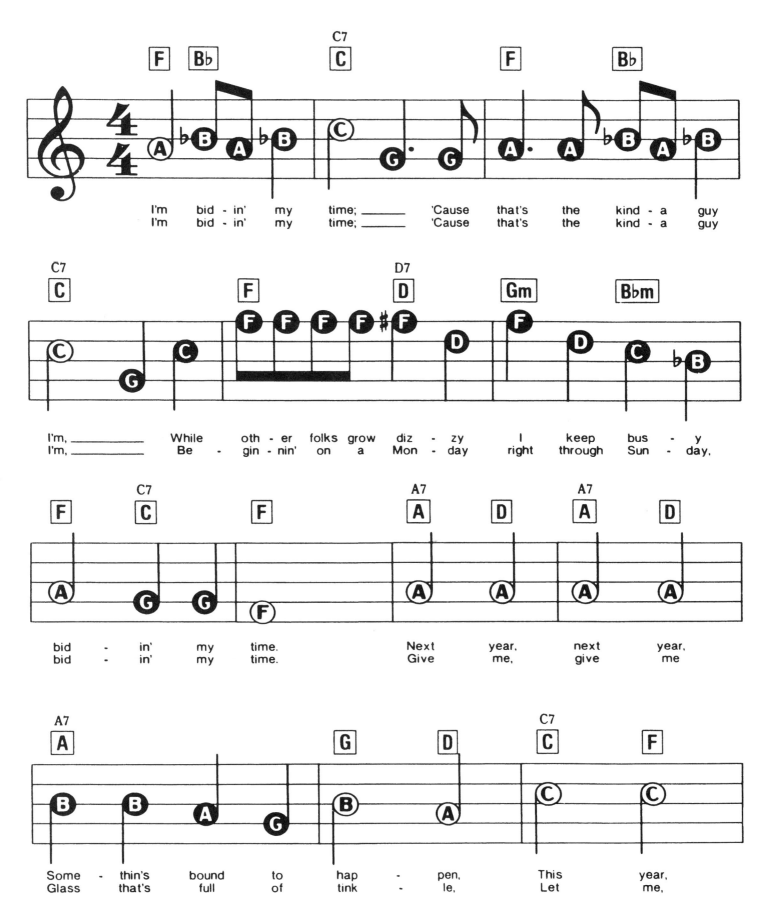

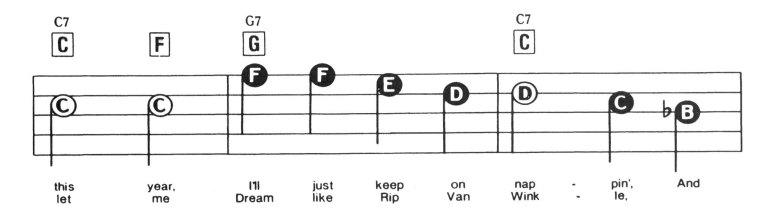

this   year,   I'll   just   keep   on   nap - pin',   And
let   me   Dream   like   Rip   Van   Wink - le,

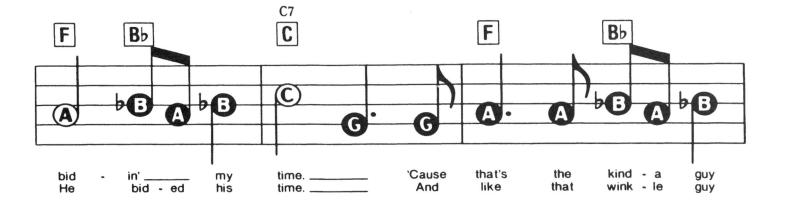

bid - in' _____ my   time. _____   'Cause   that's   the   kind - a   guy
He   bid - ed   his   time. _____   And   like   that   wink - le   guy

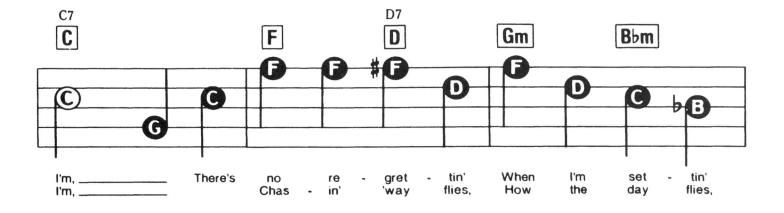

I'm, _____   There's   no   re - gret - tin'   When   I'm   set - tin'
I'm, _____   Chas - in'   'way   flies,   How   the   day   flies,

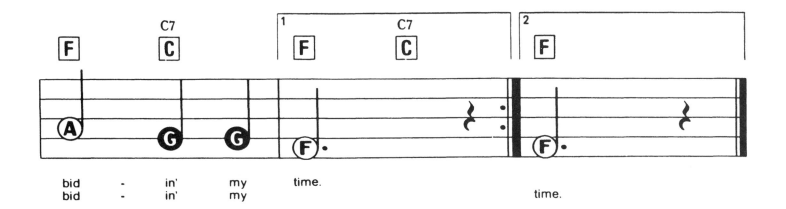

bid - in'   my   time.
bid - in'   my   time.

But Not for Me
from GIRL CRAZY

Registration 3
Rhythm: Fox Trot or Ballad

Music and Lyrics by George Gershwin
and Ira Gershwin

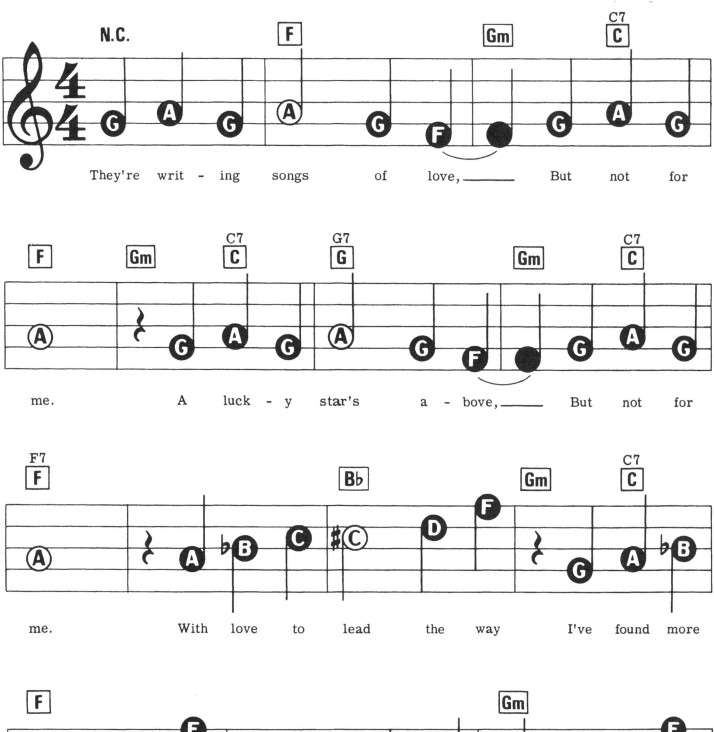

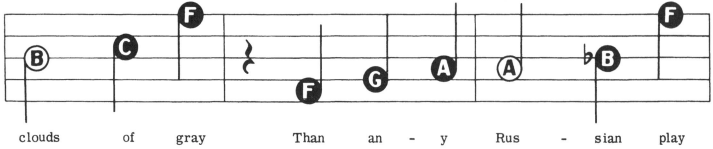

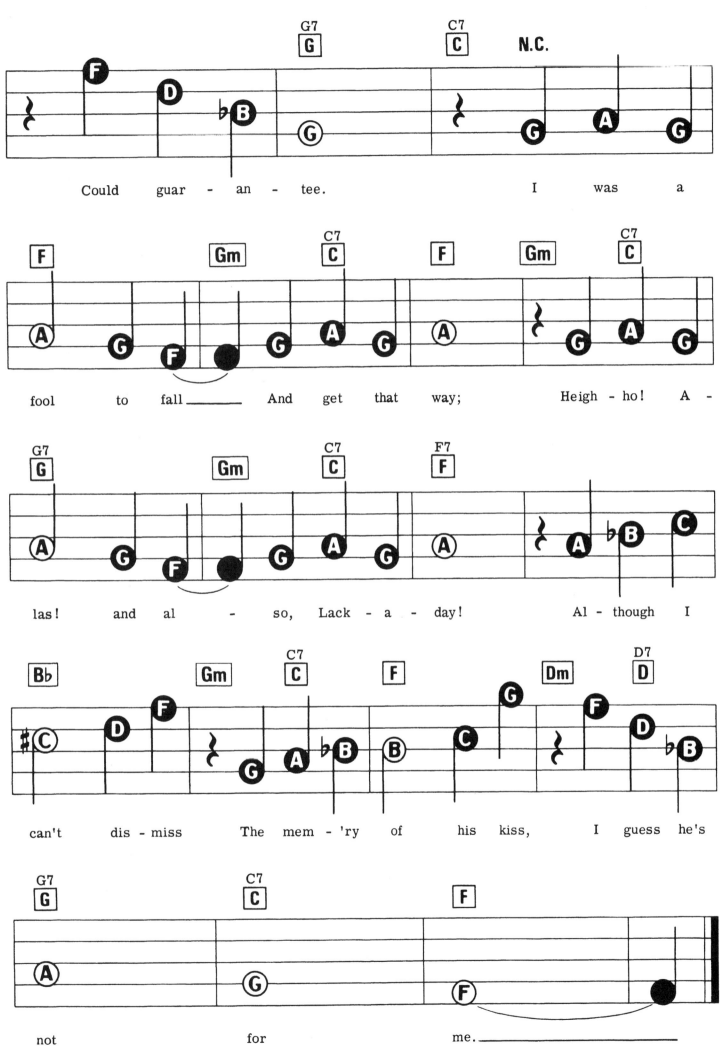

Do It Again

Registration 1
Rhythm: Fox Trot

Lyrics by B.G. DeSylva
Music by George Gershwin

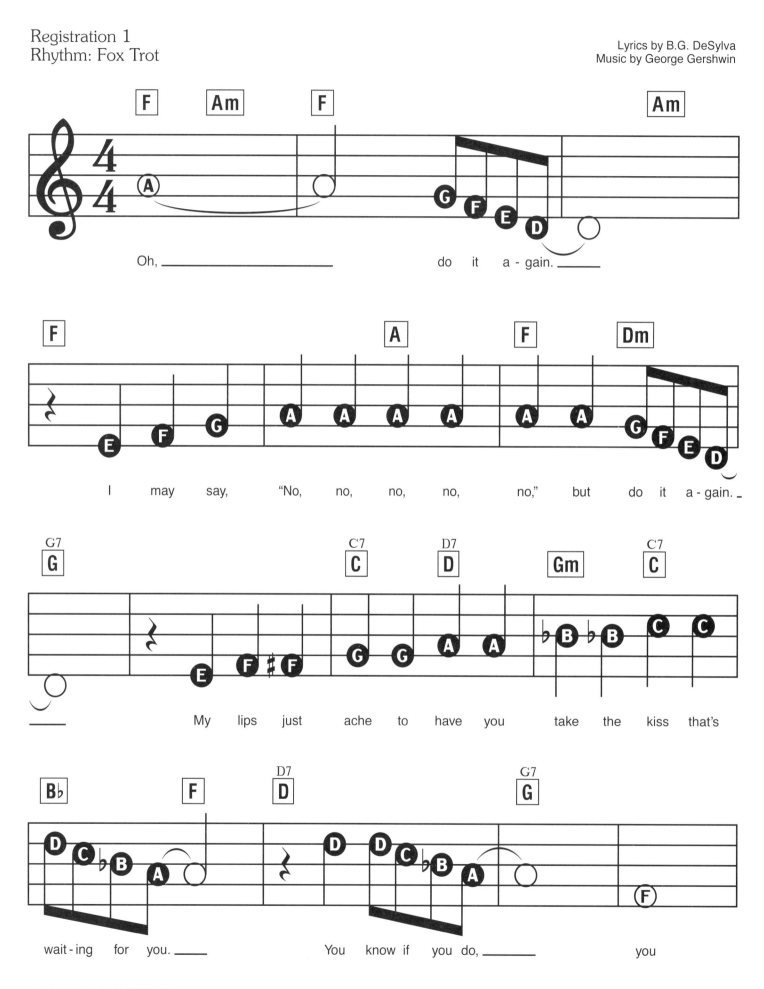

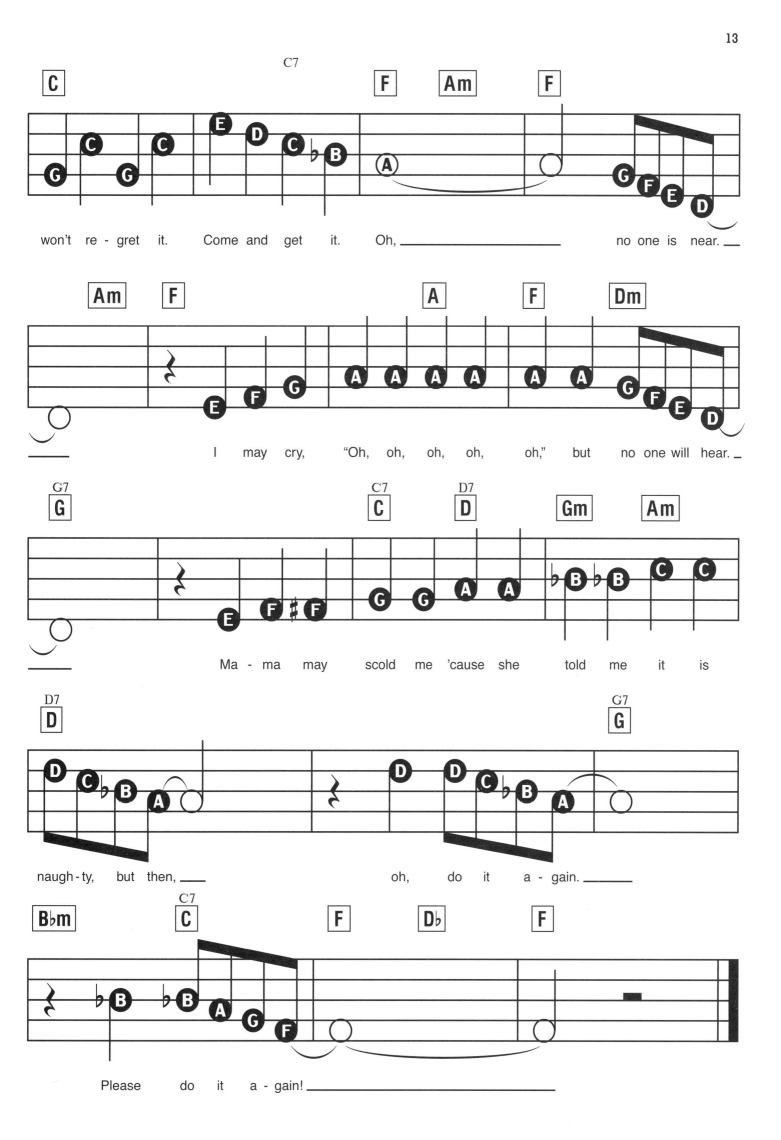

Embraceable You
from CRAZY FOR YOU

Registration 5
Rhythm: Fox Trot or Ballad

Music and Lyrics by George Gershwin
and Ira Gershwin

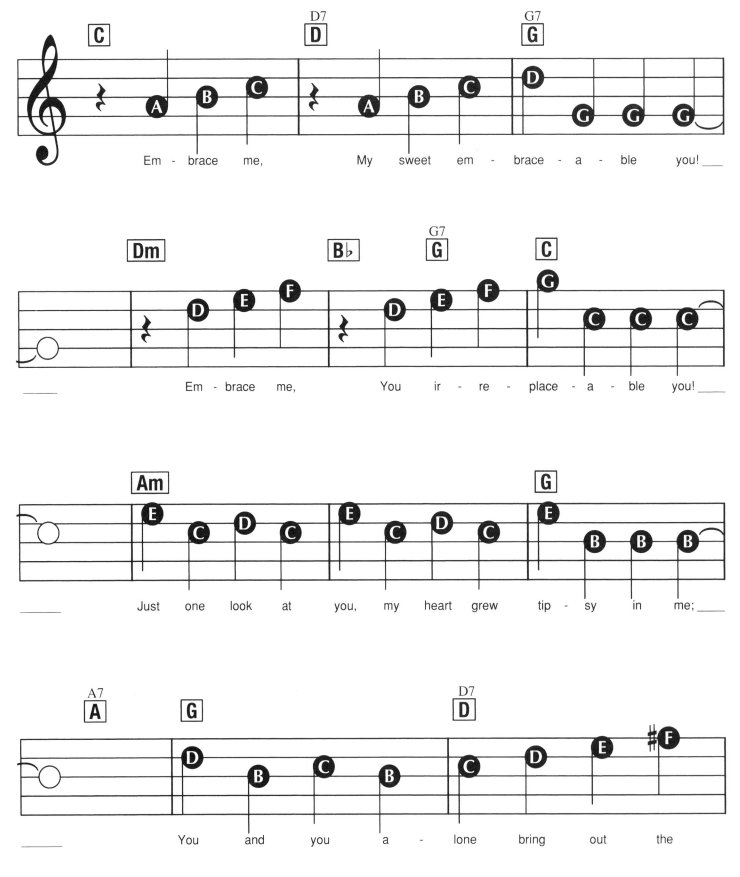

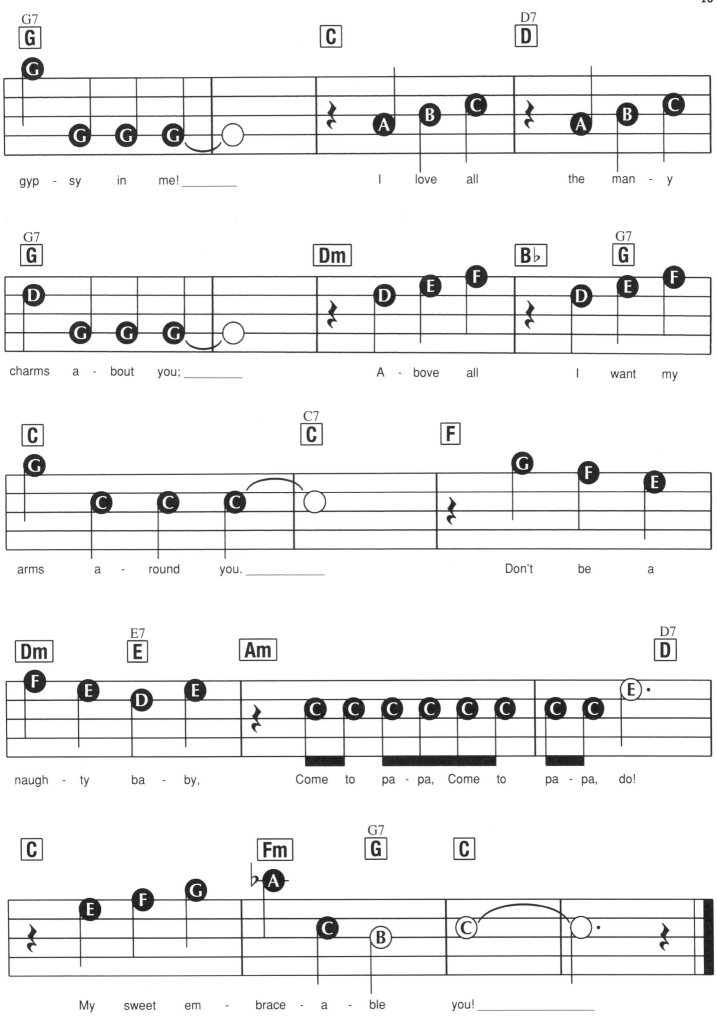

Fascinating Rhythm
from RHAPSODY IN BLUE

Registration 7
Rhythm: Fox Trot or Swing

Music and Lyrics by George Gershwin
and Ira Gershwin

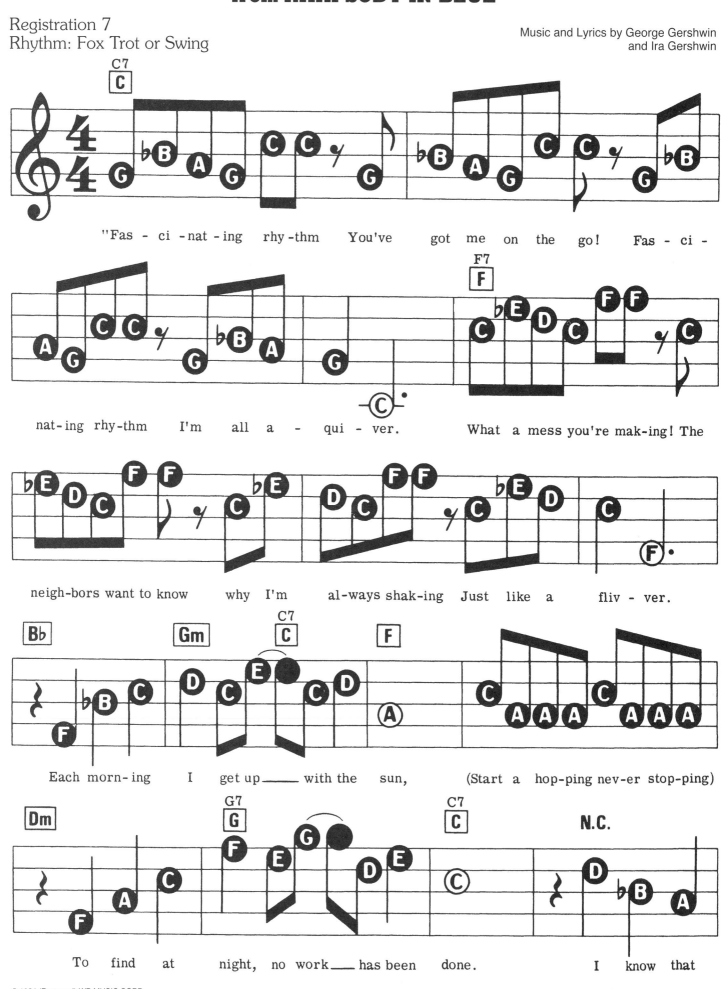

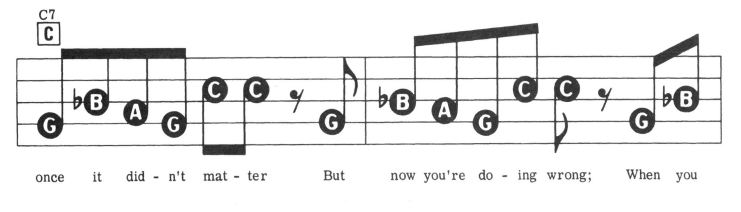

once it did-n't mat-ter   But   now you're do-ing wrong;   When you

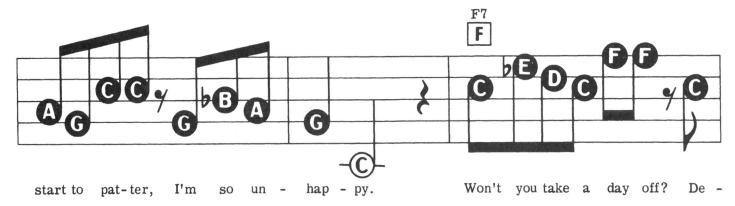

start to pat-ter, I'm so un - hap-py.   Won't you take a day off? De -

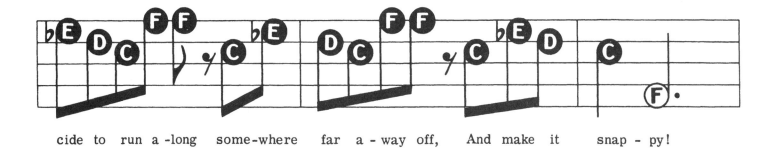

cide to run a-long some-where far a-way off, And make it snap-py!

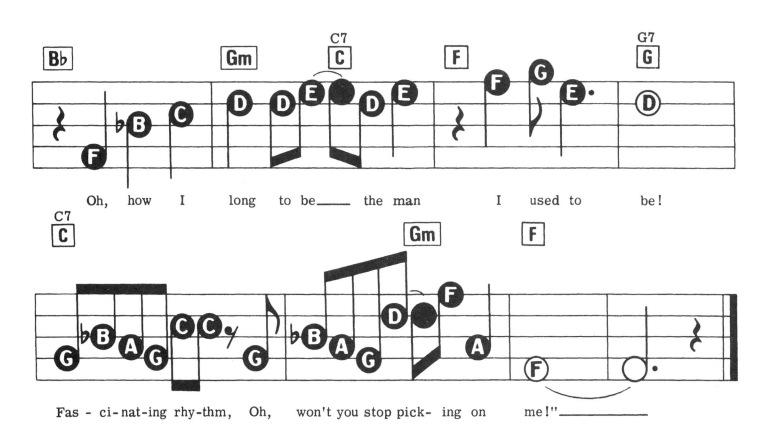

Oh, how I long to be___ the man   I used to   be!

Fas - ci-nat-ing rhy-thm, Oh, won't you stop pick-ing on   me!"_____

A Foggy Day
(In London Town)
from A DAMSEL IN DISTRESS

Registration 5
Rhythm: Swing or Fox Trot

Music and Lyrics by George Gershwin
and Ira Gershwin

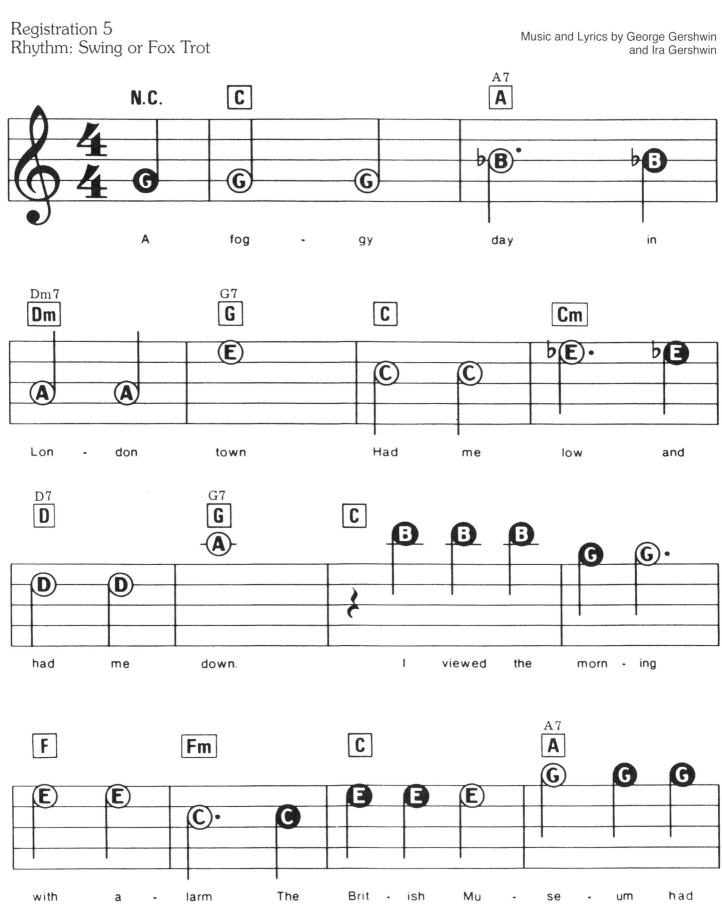

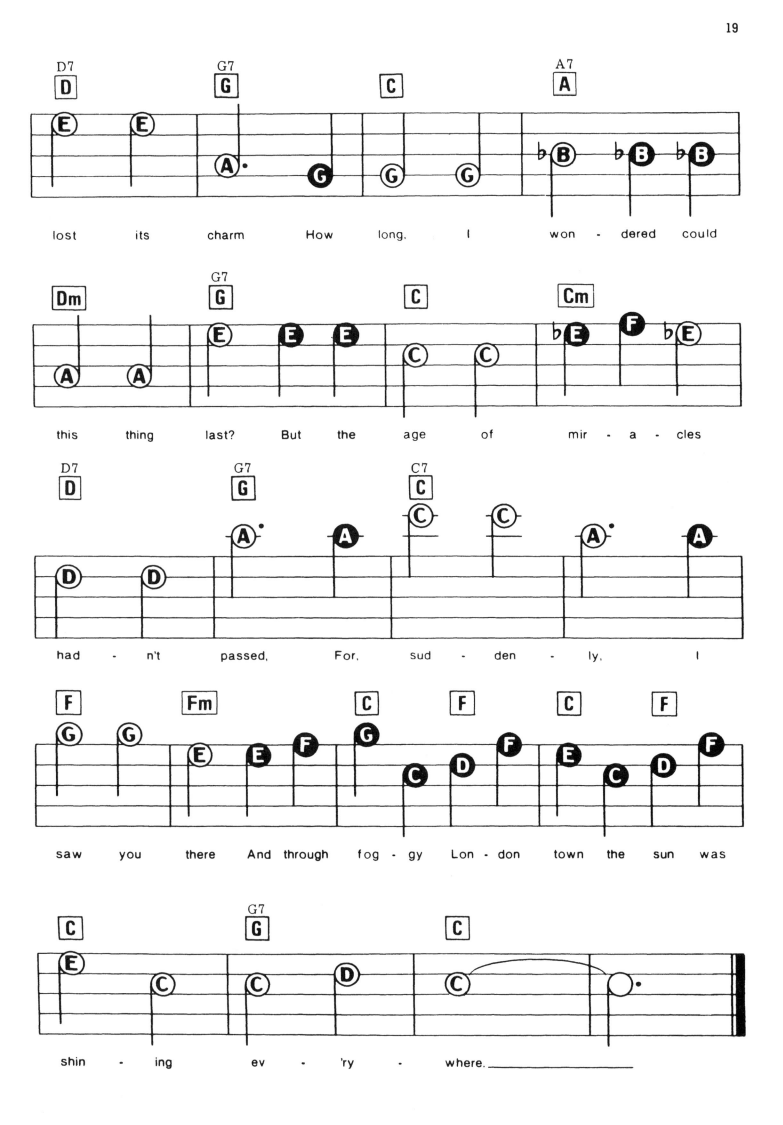

For You, For Me For Evermore

Registration 5
Rhythm: Ballad

Music and Lyrics by George Gershwin
and Ira Gershwin

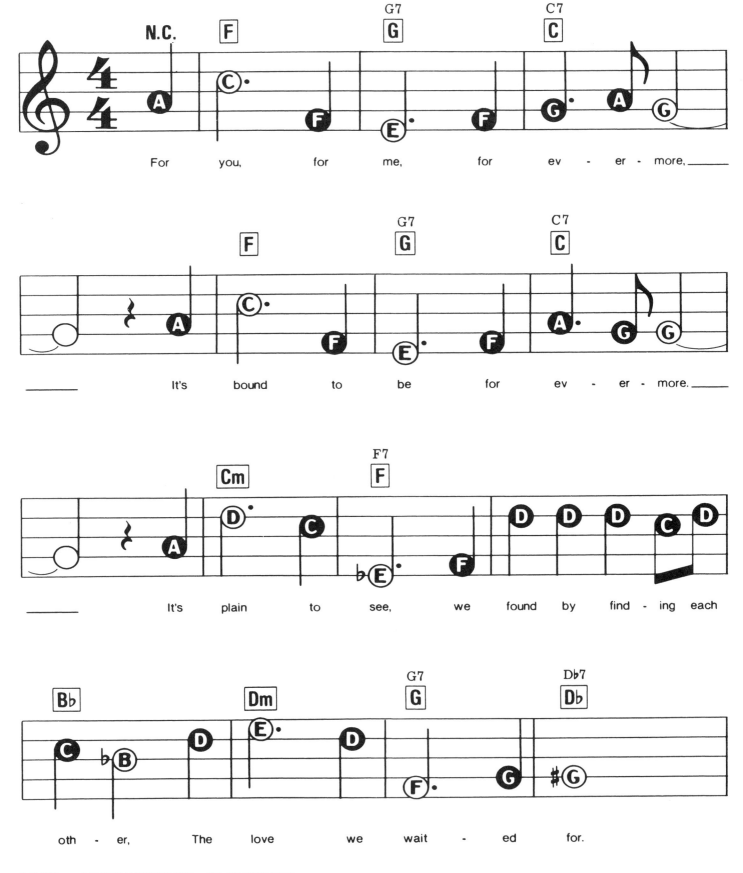

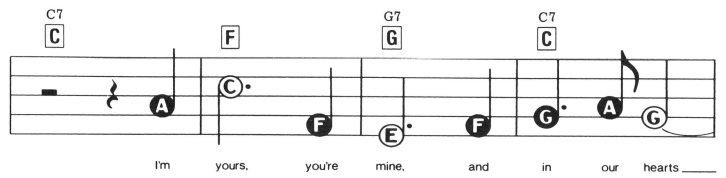

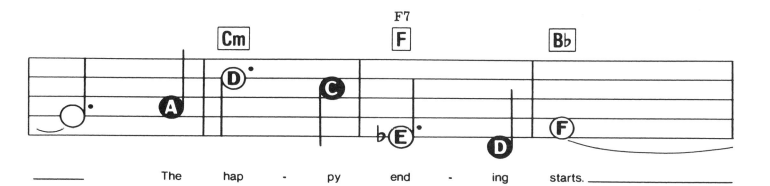

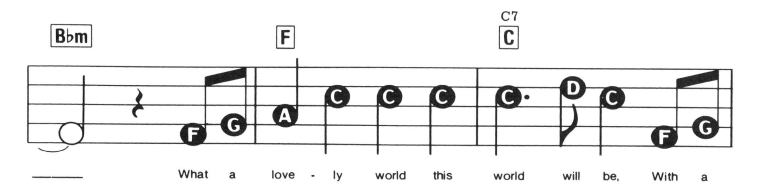

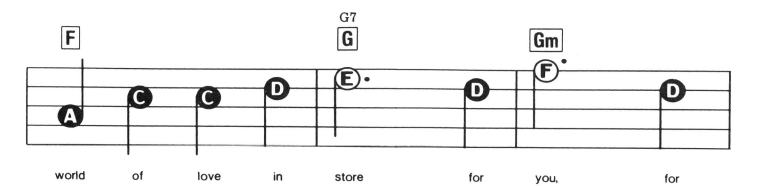

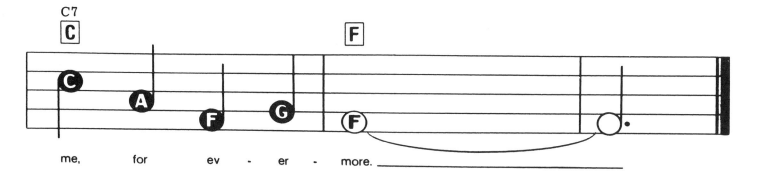

He Loves and She Loves

from FUNNY FACE

Registration 1
Rhythm: Ballad or Fox Trot

Words and Music by George Gershwin
and Ira Gershwin

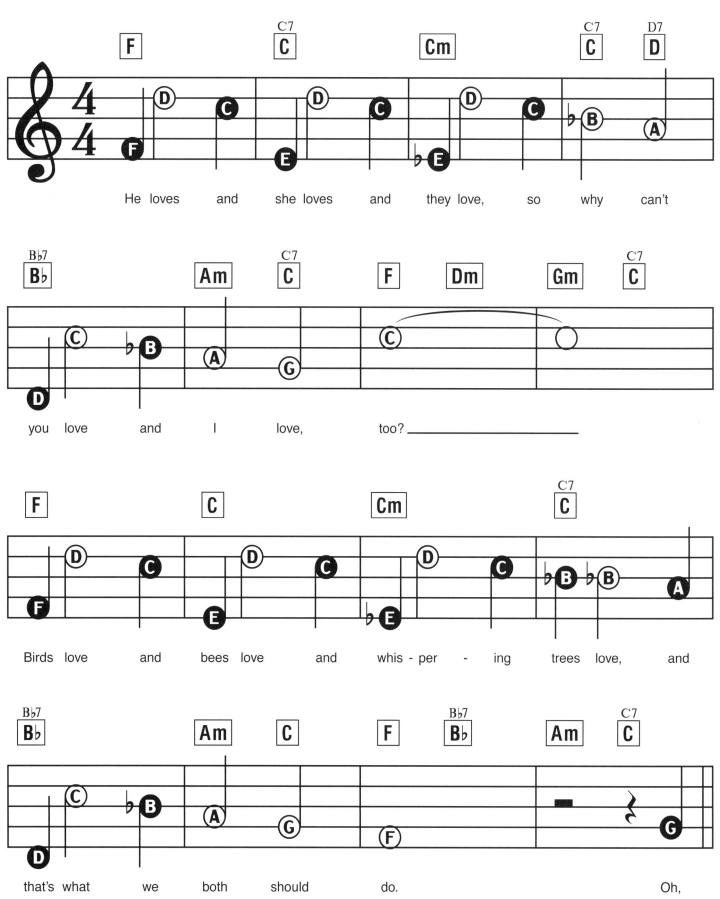

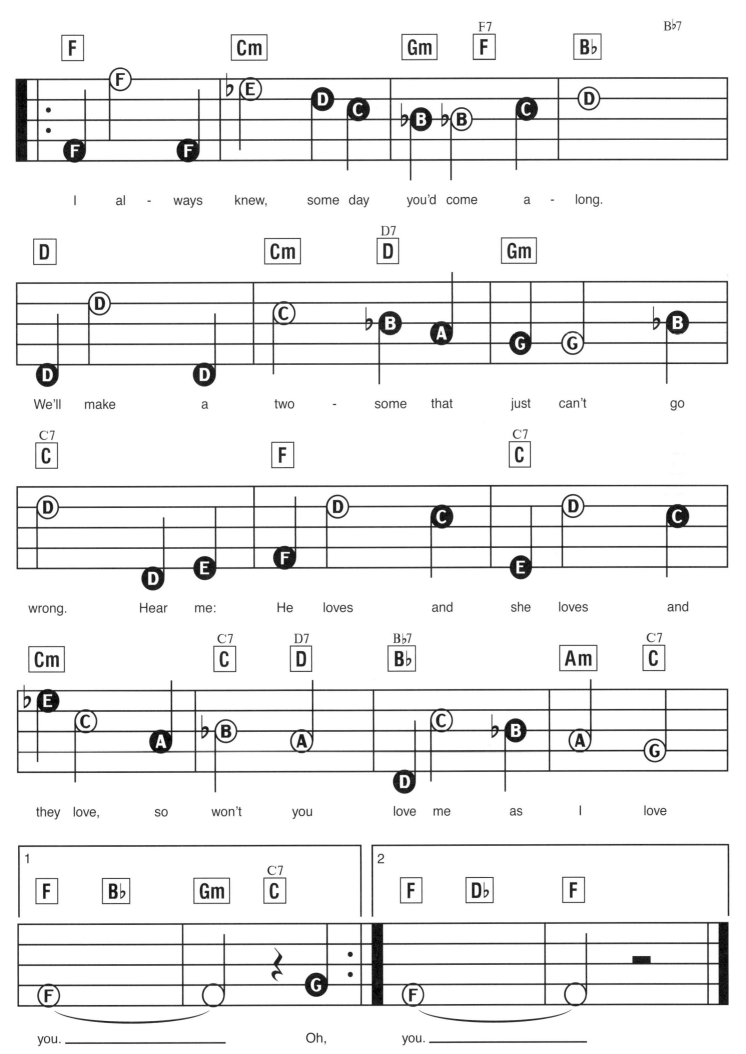

How Long Has This Been Going On?

Registration 2
Rhythm: Swing or Jazz

Music and Lyrics by George Gershwin
and Ira Gershwin

I Got Rhythm
from AN AMERICAN IN PARIS
from GIRL CRAZY

Registration 7
Rhythm: Fox Trot or Swing

Music and Lyrics by George Gershwin
and Ira Gershwin

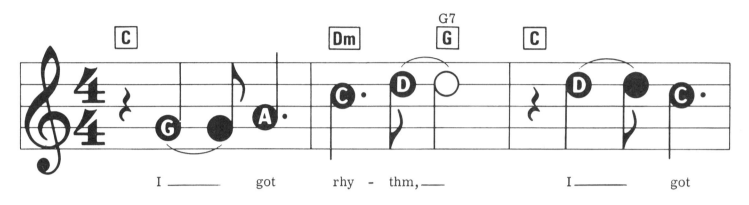

I _____ got rhy - thm, _____ I _____ got

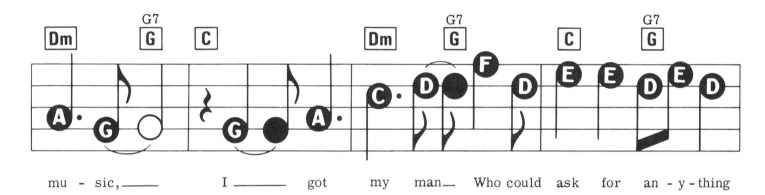

mu - sic, _____ I _____ got my man _____ Who could ask for an - y - thing

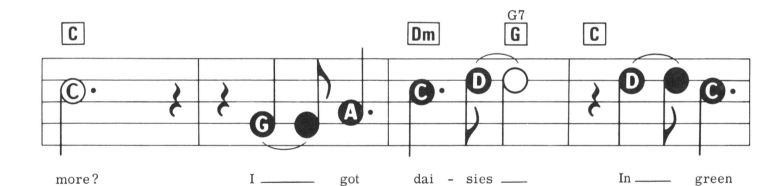

more? I _____ got dai - sies _____ In _____ green

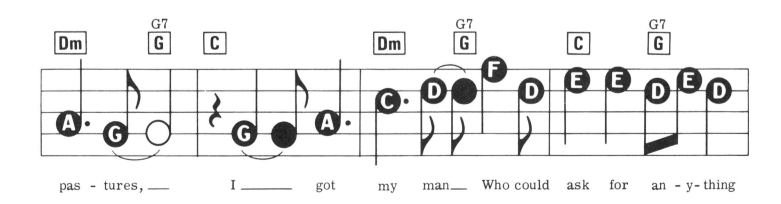

pas - tures, _____ I _____ got my man _____ Who could ask for an - y - thing

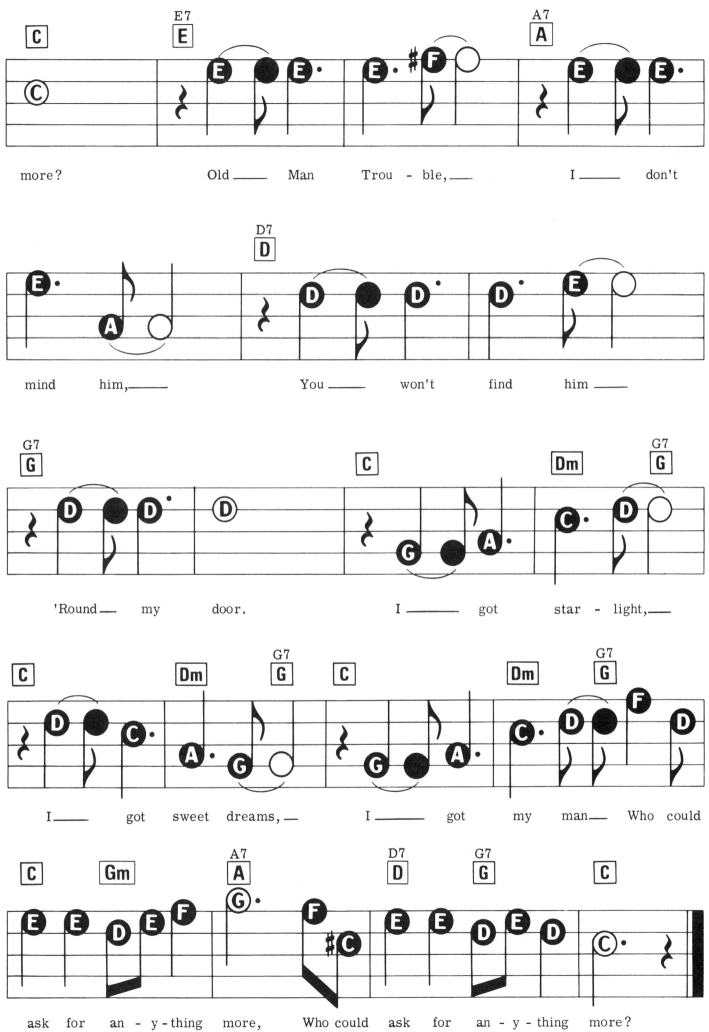

I Was Doing All Right

Registration 2
Rhythm: Fox Trot

Words and Music by George Gershwin
and Ira Gershwin

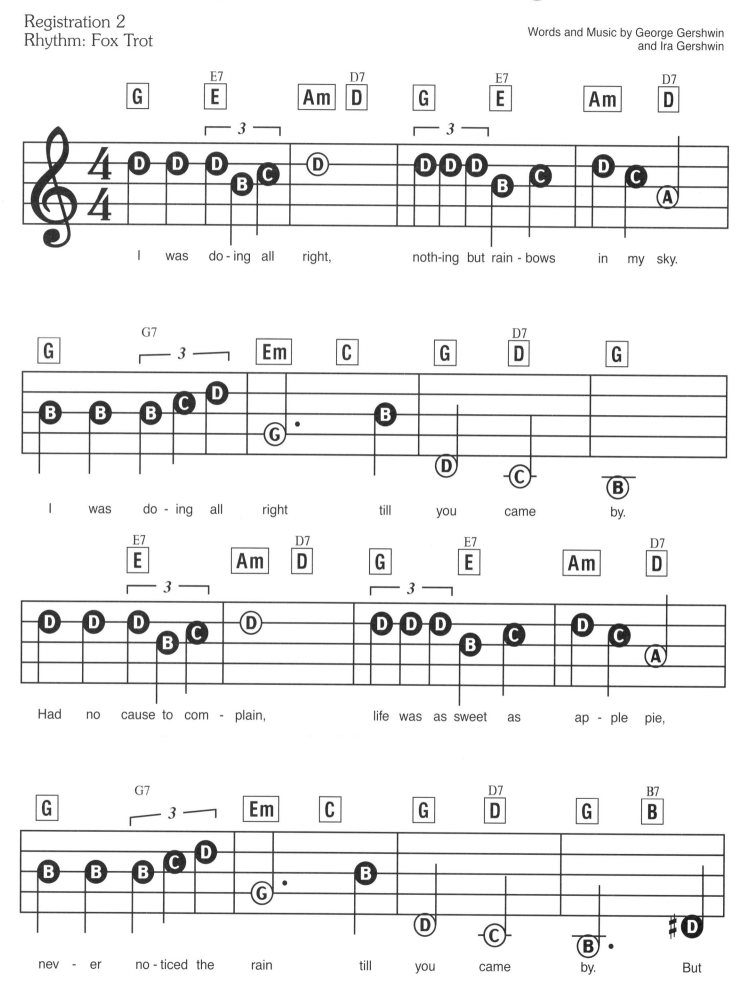

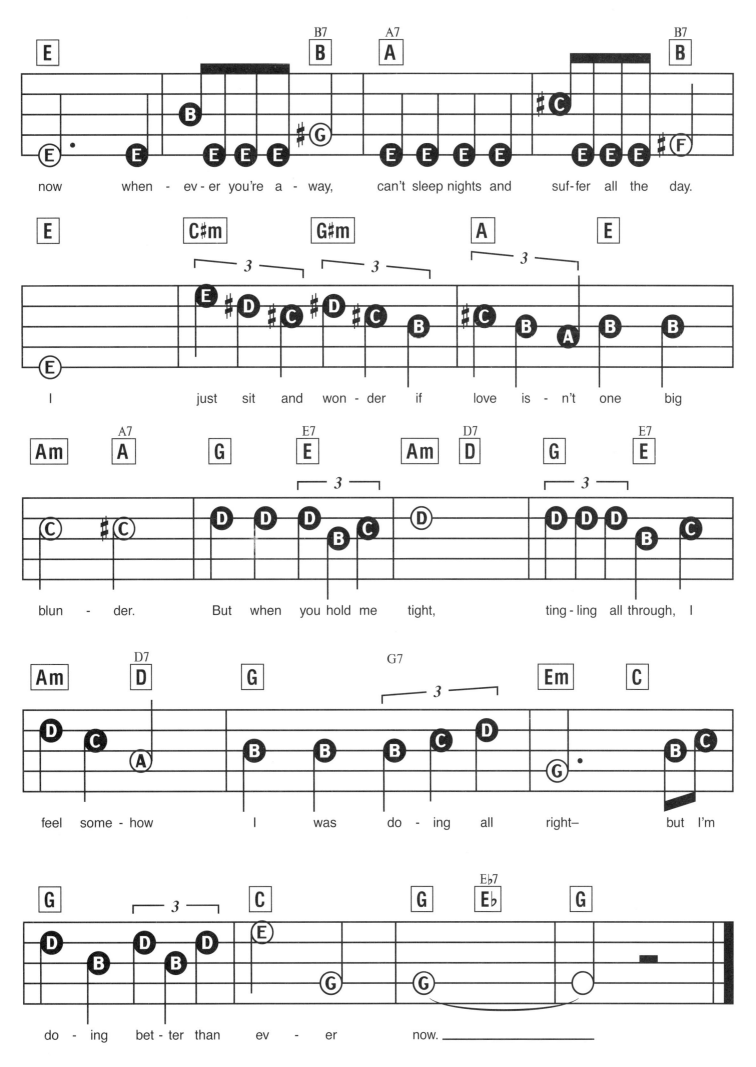

I've Got a Crush on You
from STRIKE UP THE BAND

Registration 5
Rhythm: Fox Trot or Ballad

Music and Lyrics by George Gershwin
and Ira Gershwin

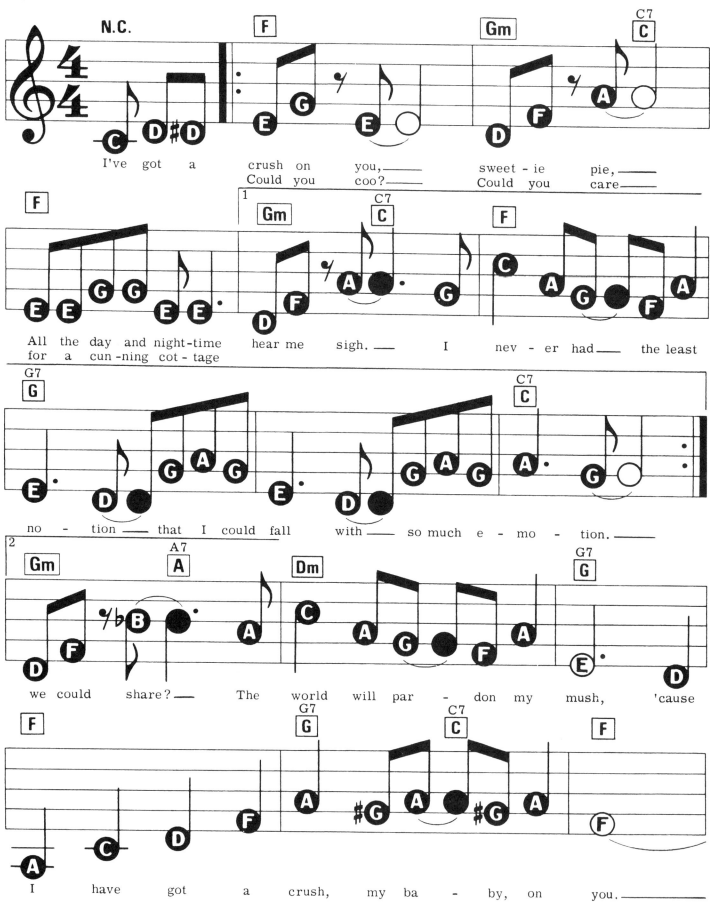

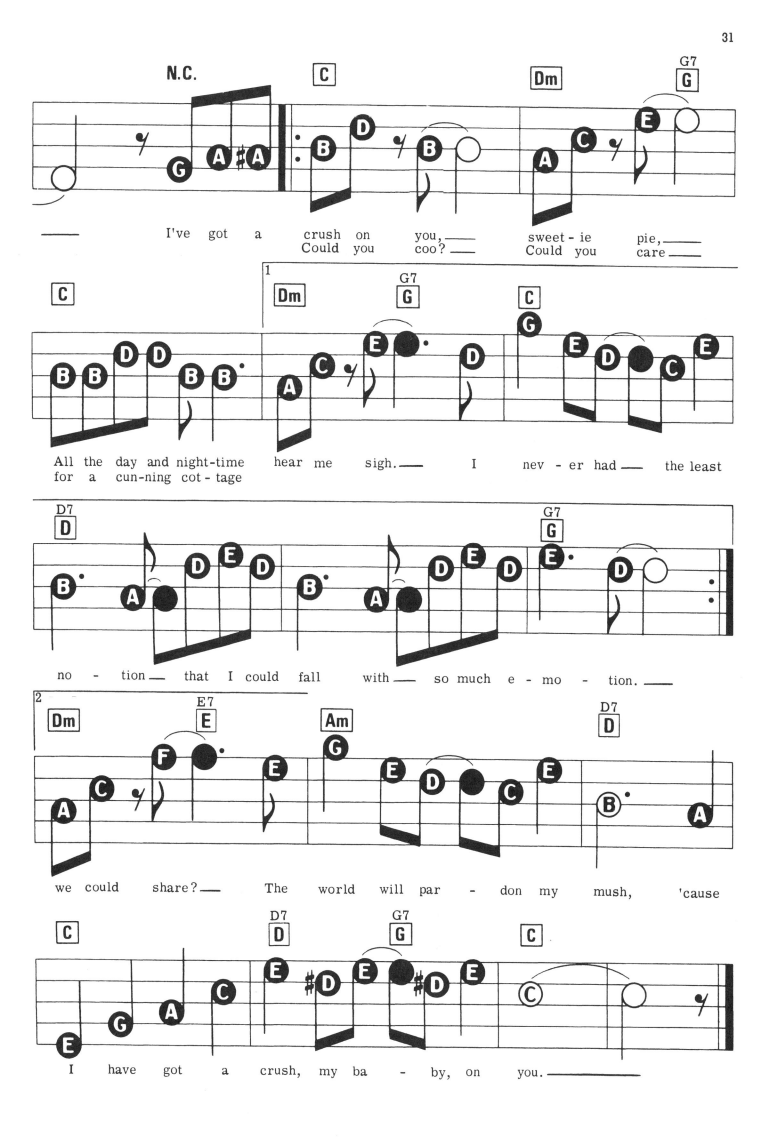

Isn't It a Pity

Registration 3
Rhythm: Ballad

Words and Music by George Gershwin
and Ira Gershwin

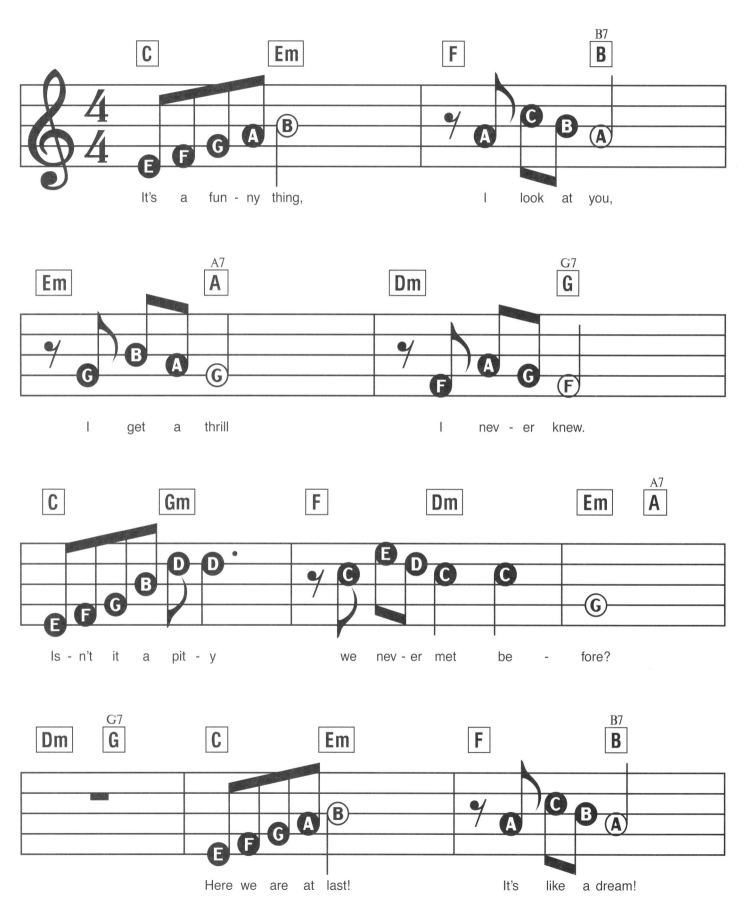

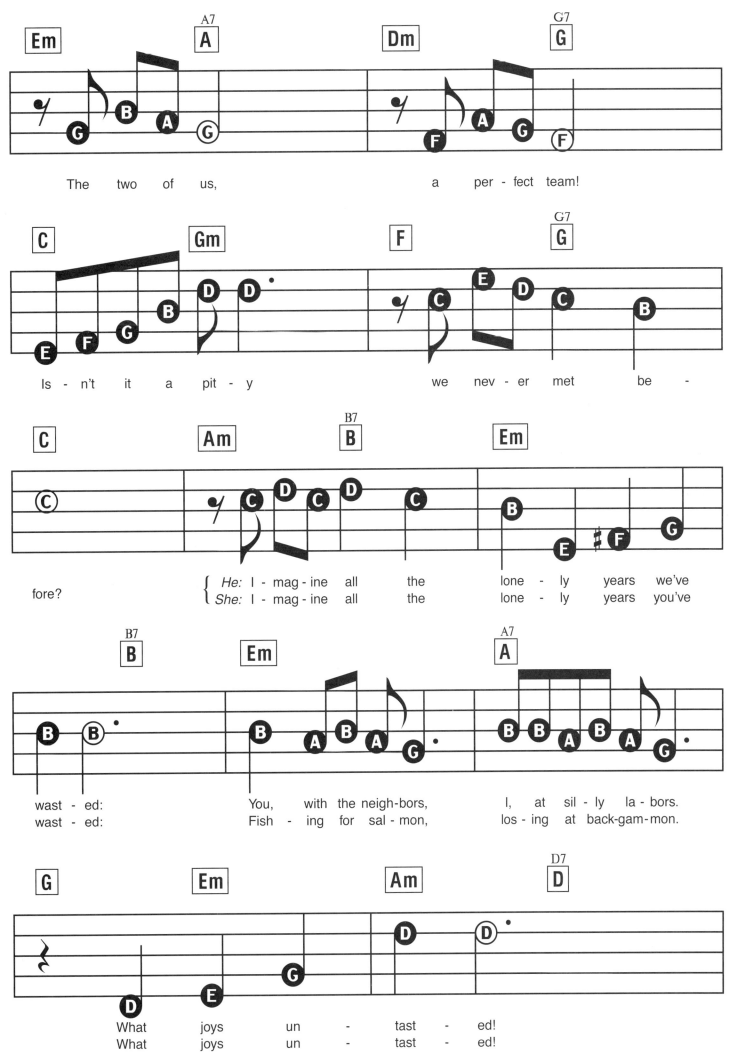

Let's Call the Whole Thing Off
from SHALL WE DANCE

Registration 1
Rhythm: Swing

Music and Lyrics by George Gershwin
and Ira Gershwin

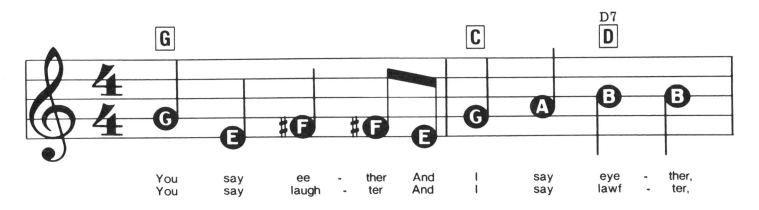

You say ee - ther And I say eye - ther,
You say laugh - ter And I say lawf - ter,

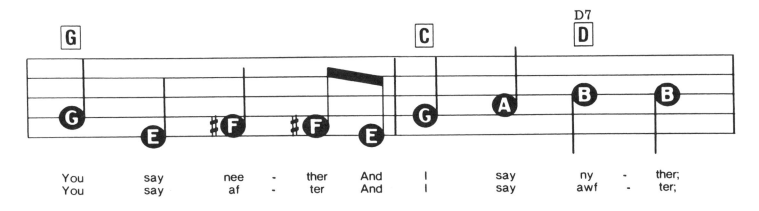

You say nee - ther And I say ny - ther;
You say af - ter And I say awf - ter;

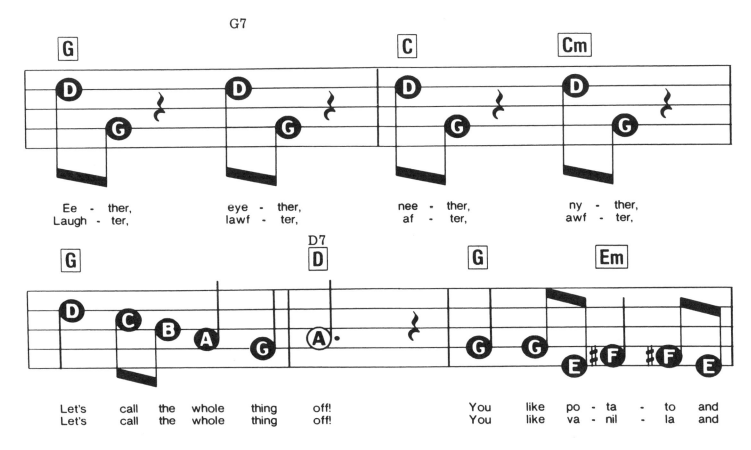

Ee - ther, eye - ther, nee - ther, ny - ther,
Laugh - ter, lawf - ter, af - ter, awf - ter,

Let's call the whole thing off! You like po - ta - to and
Let's call the whole thing off! You like va - nil - la and

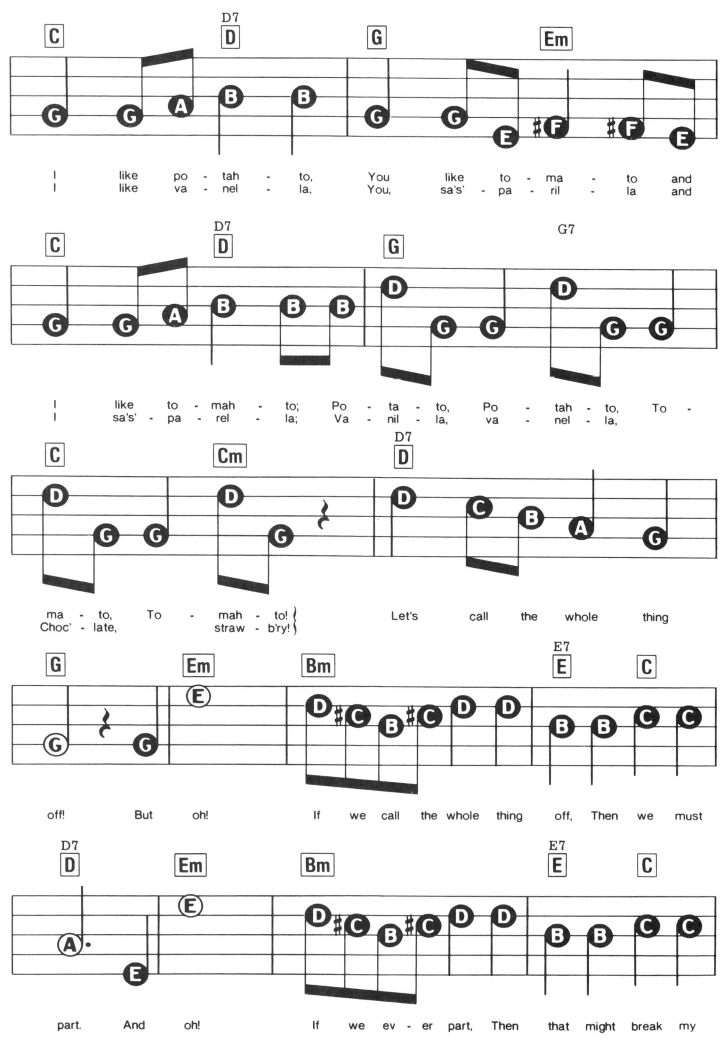

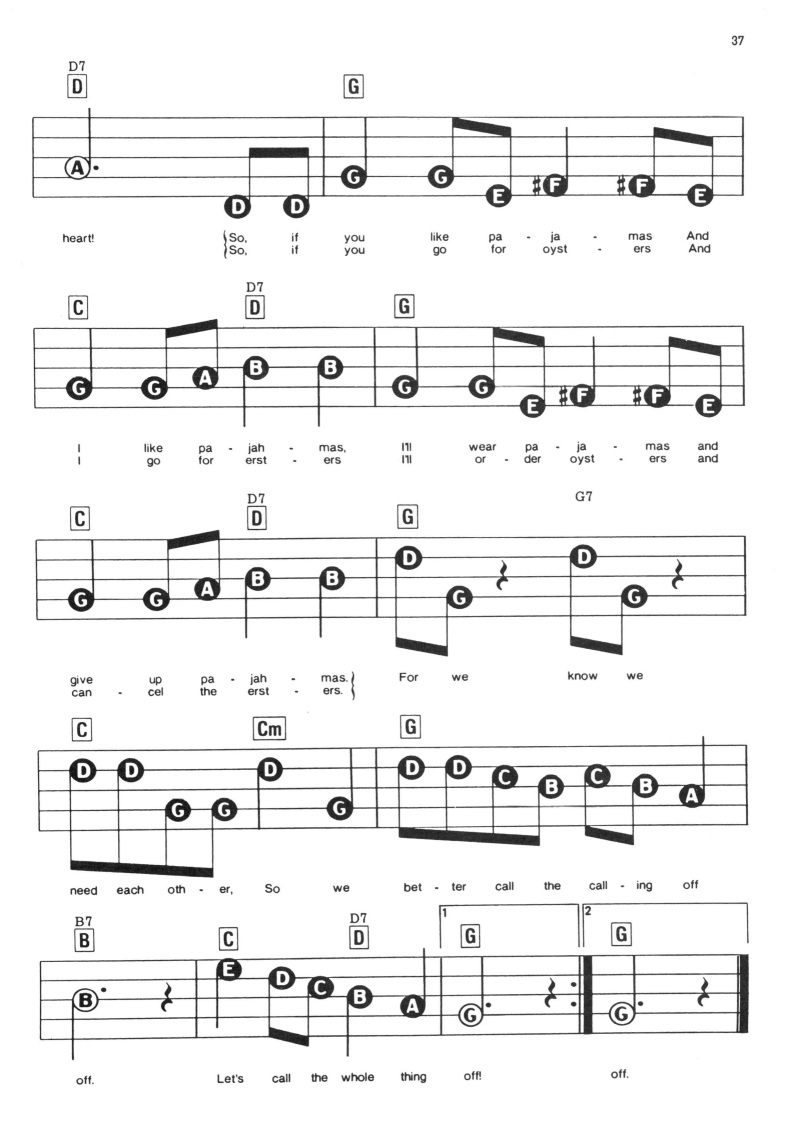

It Ain't Necessarily So
from PORGY AND BESS

Registration 7
Rhythm: Ballad

Music and Lyrics by George Gershwin,
Du Bose and Dorothy Heyward
and Ira Gershwin

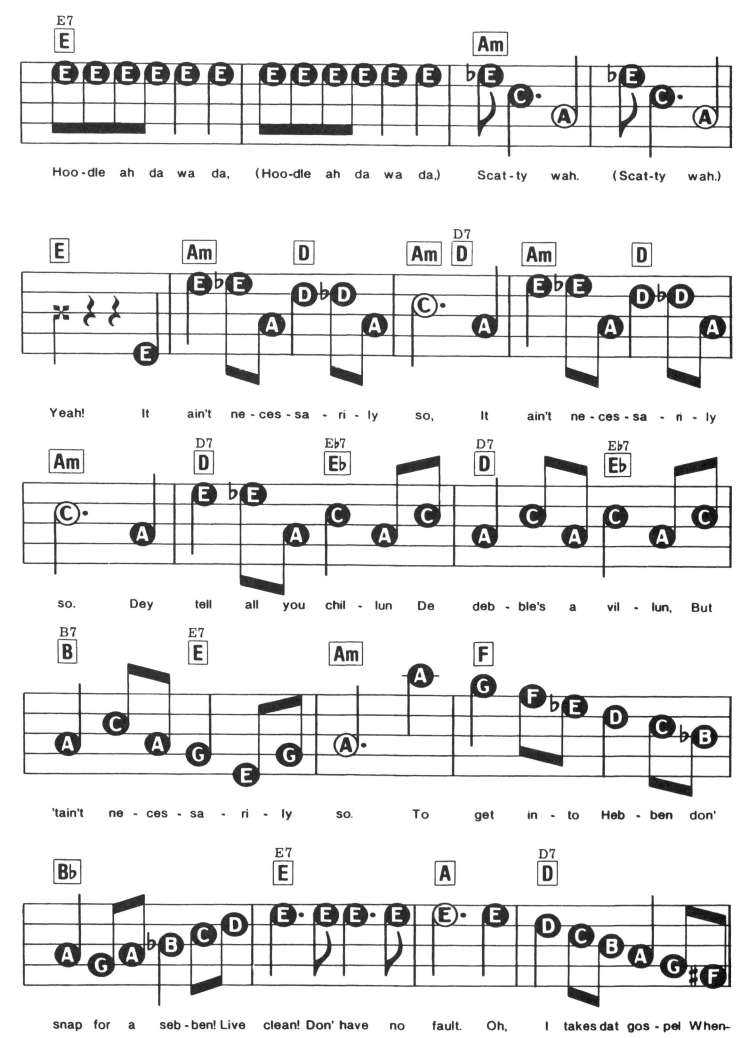

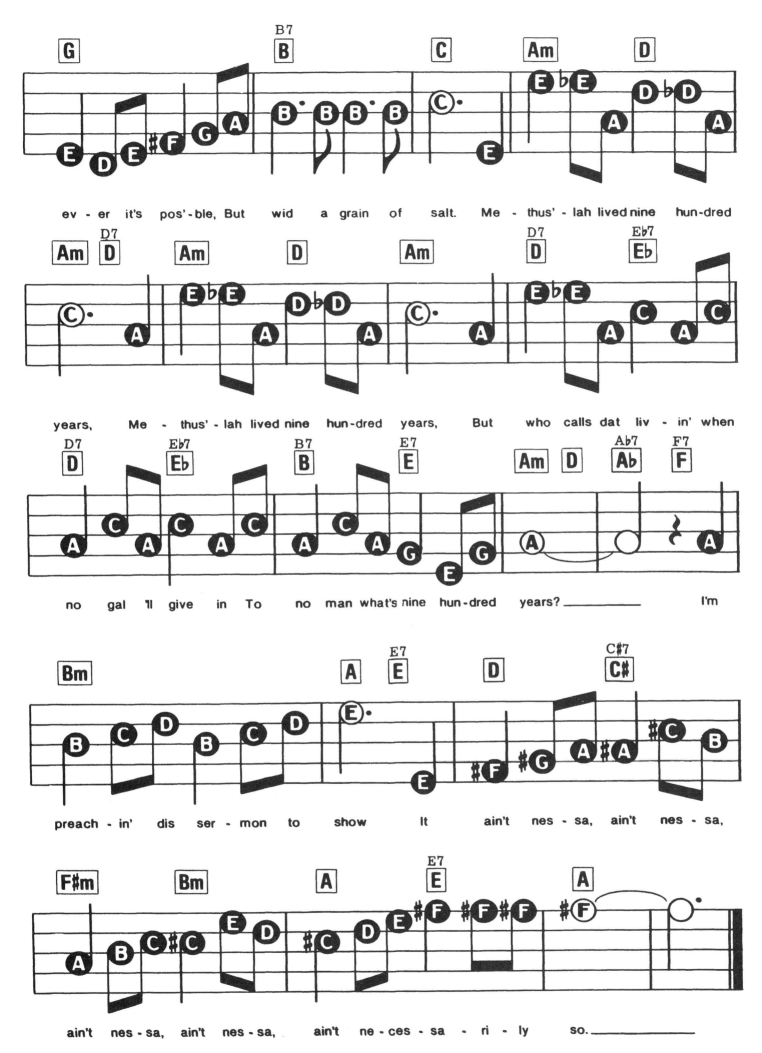

Little Jazz Bird

Registration 7
Rhythm: Swing

Words and Music by George Gershwin
and Ira Gershwin

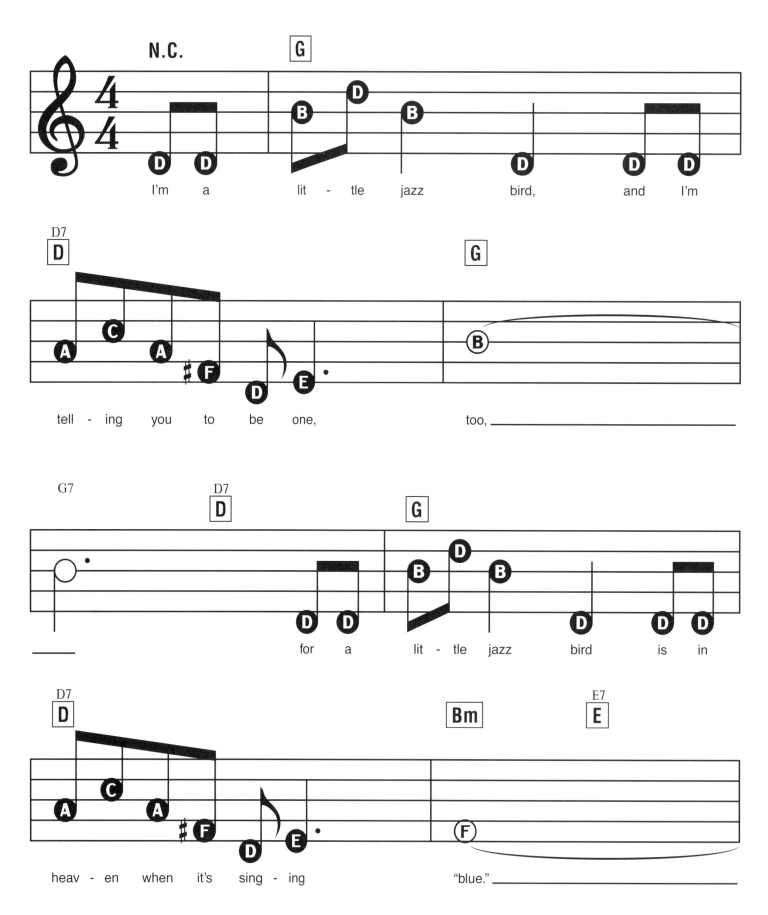

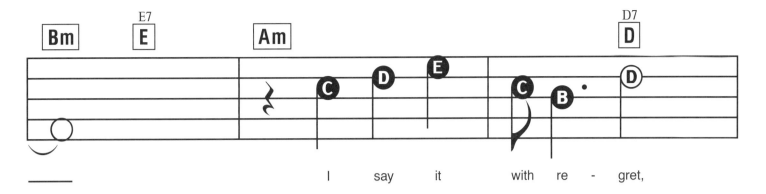

I say it with re - gret,

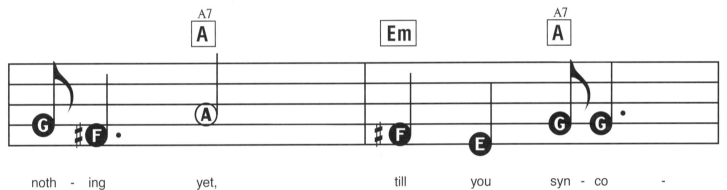

but you're out of date; you ain't heard

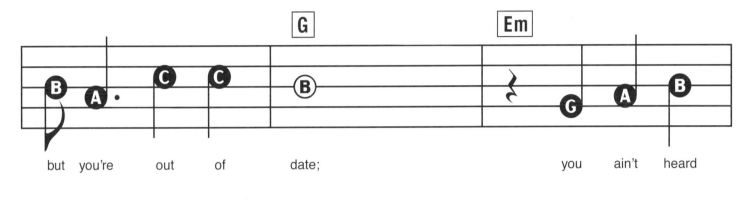

noth - ing yet, till you syn - co -

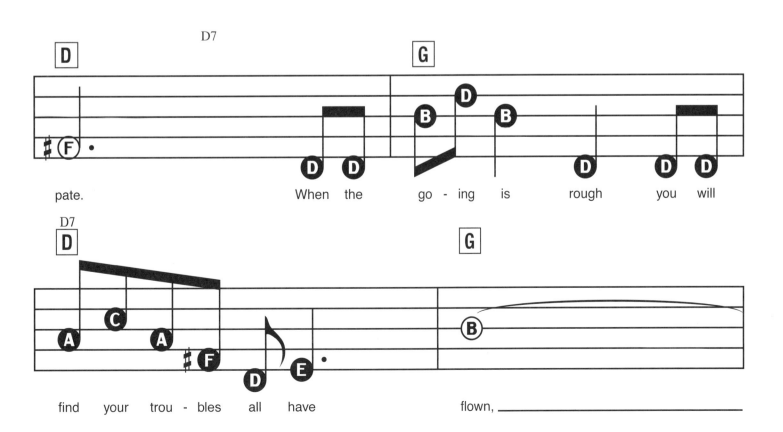

pate. When the go - ing is rough you will

find your trou - bles all have flown, _____

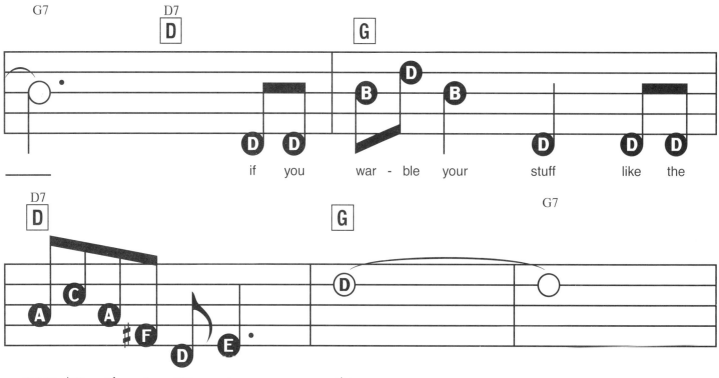

if you war - ble your stuff like the

moan - ing of a sax - o - phone. _____

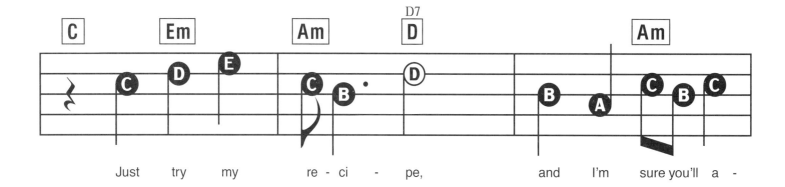

Just try my re - ci - pe, and I'm sure you'll a -

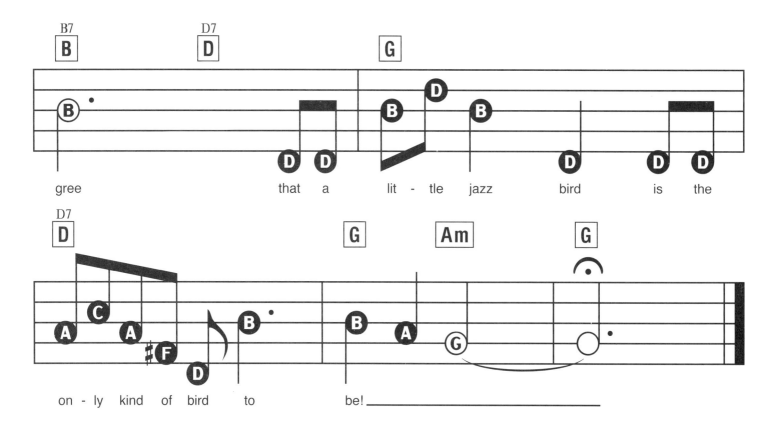

gree that a lit - tle jazz bird is the

on - ly kind of bird to be! _____

Love Is Sweeping the Country

Registration 5
Rhythm: Fox Trot or Swing

Music and Lyrics by George Gershwin
and Ira Gershwin

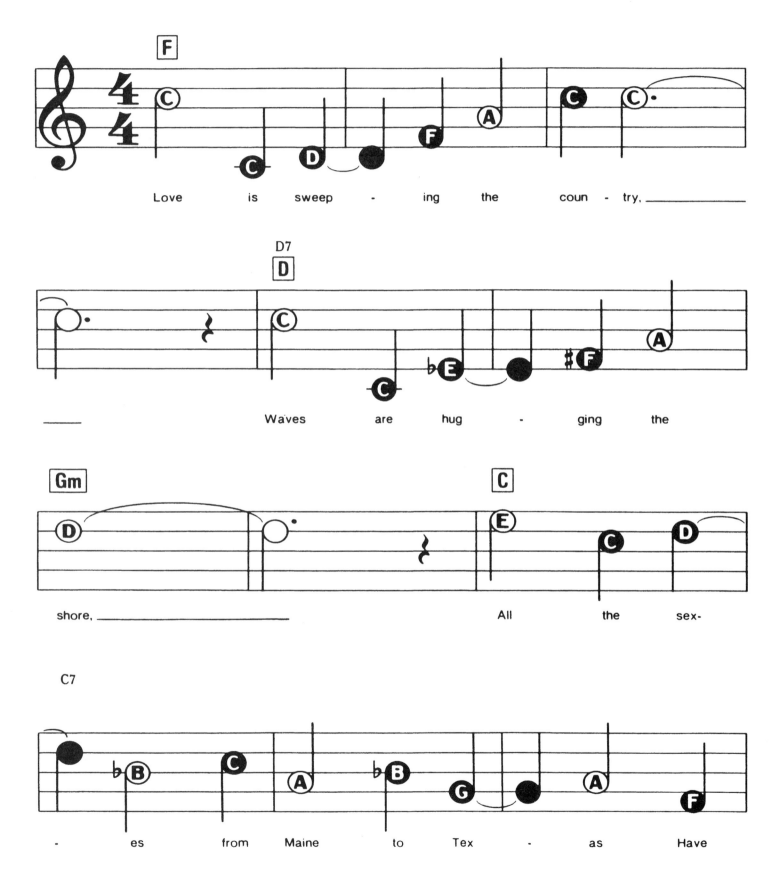

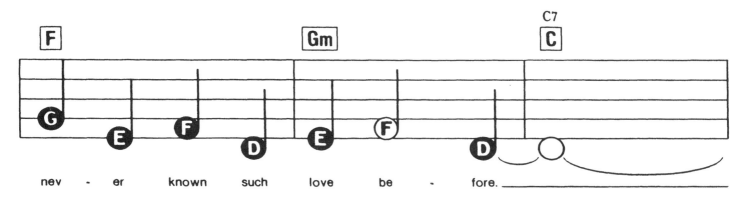

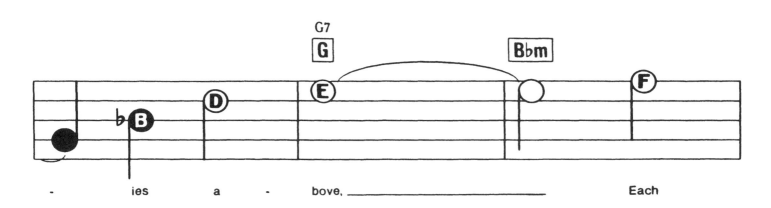

F7

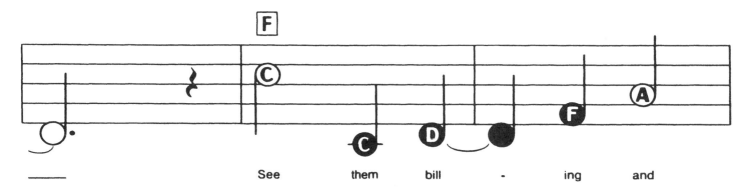

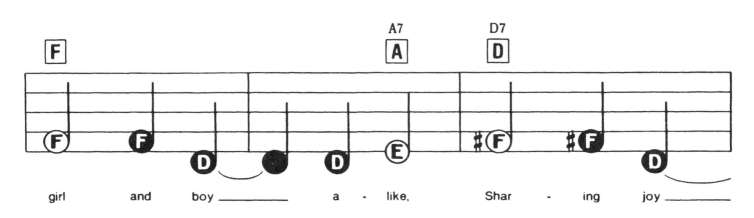

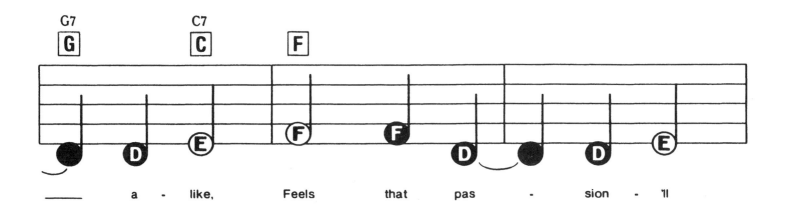

_____ a - like, Feels that pas - sion - 'll

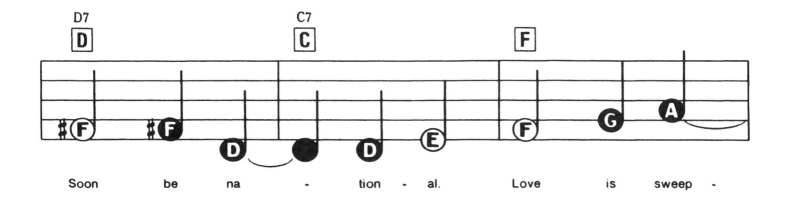

Soon be na - tion - al. Love is sweep -

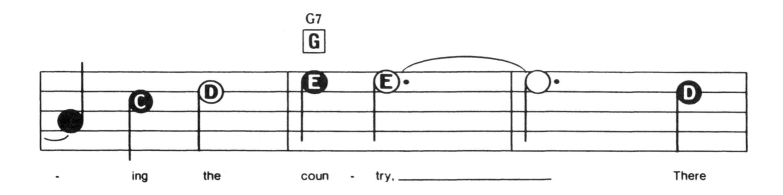

- ing the coun - try, _____ There

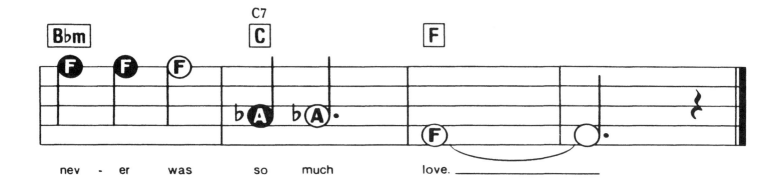

nev - er was so much love. _____

Liza
(All the Clouds'll Roll Away)

Registration 3
Rhythm: Fox Trot or Swing

Music by George Gershwin
Lyrics by Ira Gershwin and Gus Kahn

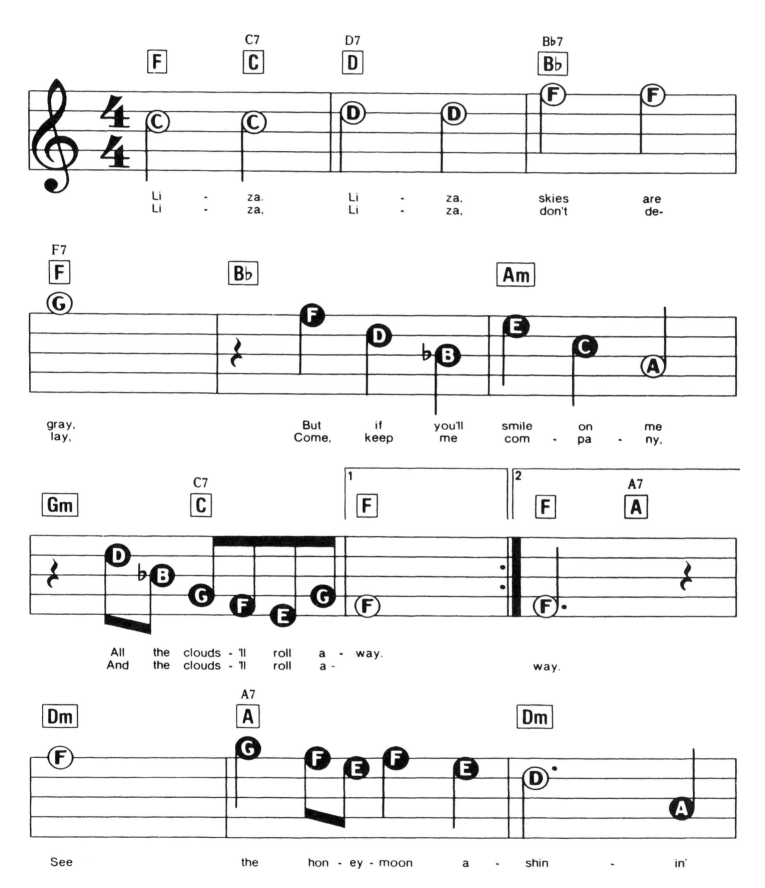

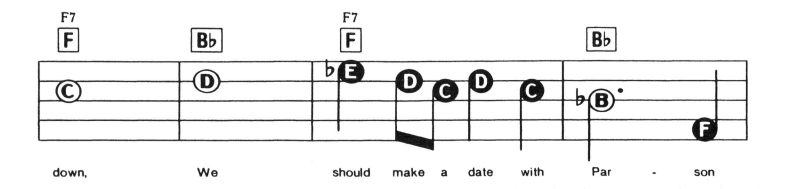

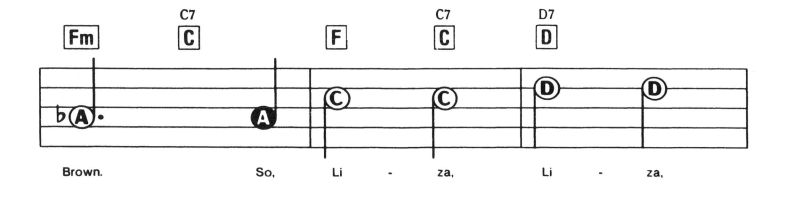

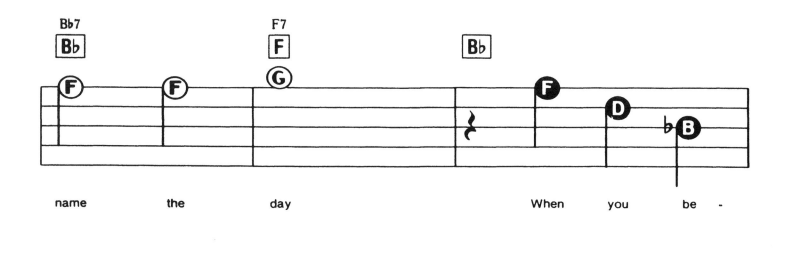

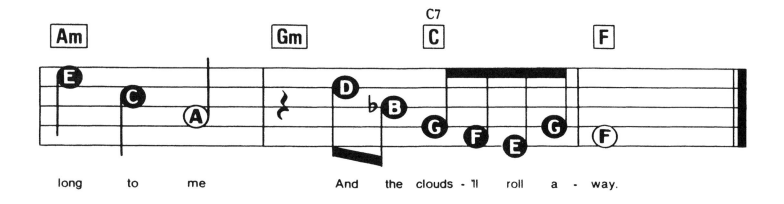

49

Looking for a Boy

Registration 5
Rhythm: Fox Trot or Swing

Music and Lyrics by George Gershwin
and Ira Gershwin

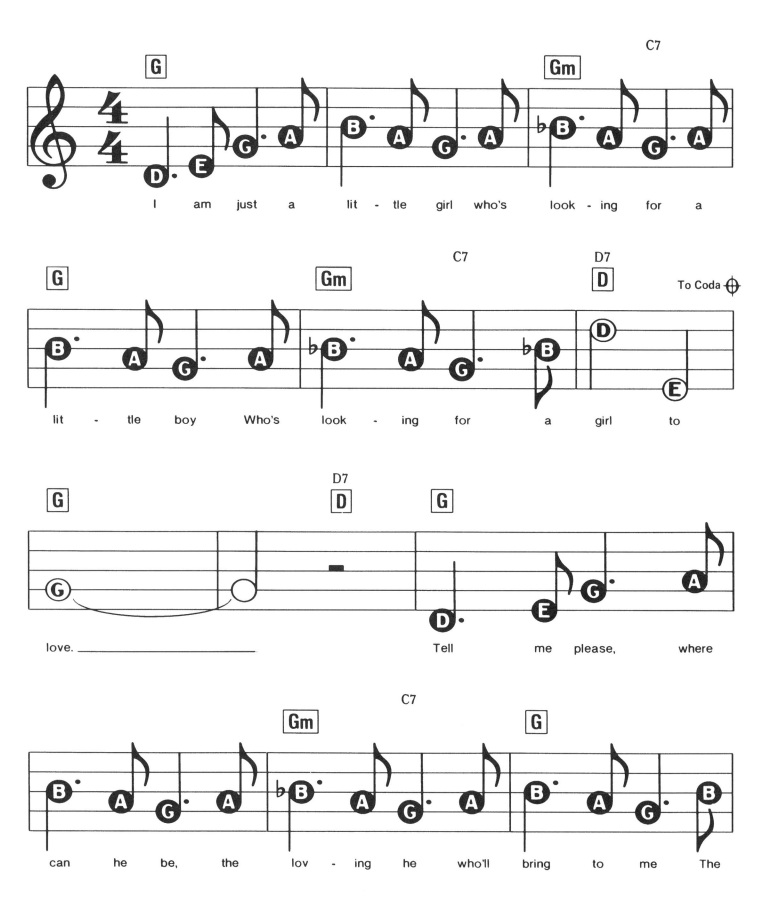

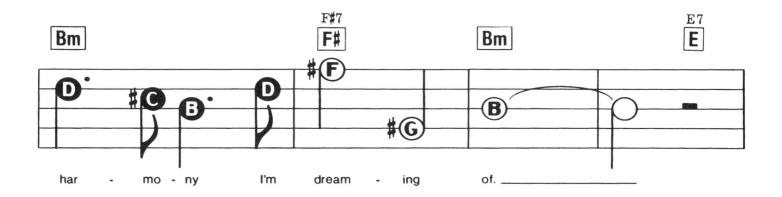

har - mo - ny   I'm   dream - ing   of. _____

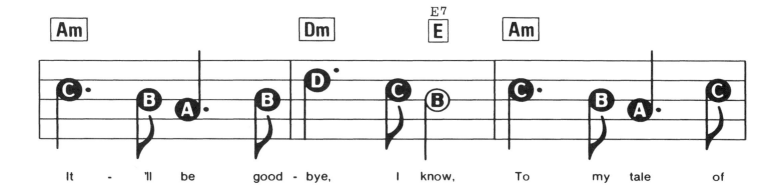

It - 'll   be   good - bye,   I   know,   To   my   tale   of

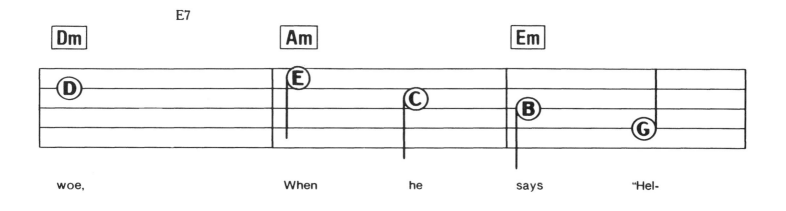

woe,   When   he   says   "Hel-

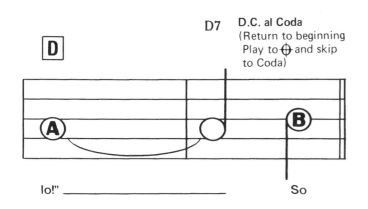

lo!" _____   So

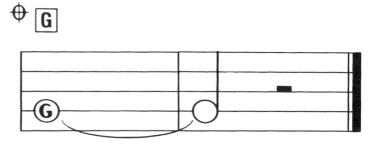

love. _____

Love Is Here to Stay
from GOLDWYN FOLLIES
from AN AMERICAN IN PARIS

Registration 4
Rhythm: Fox Trot or Ballad

Music and Lyrics by George Gershwin
and Ira Gershwin

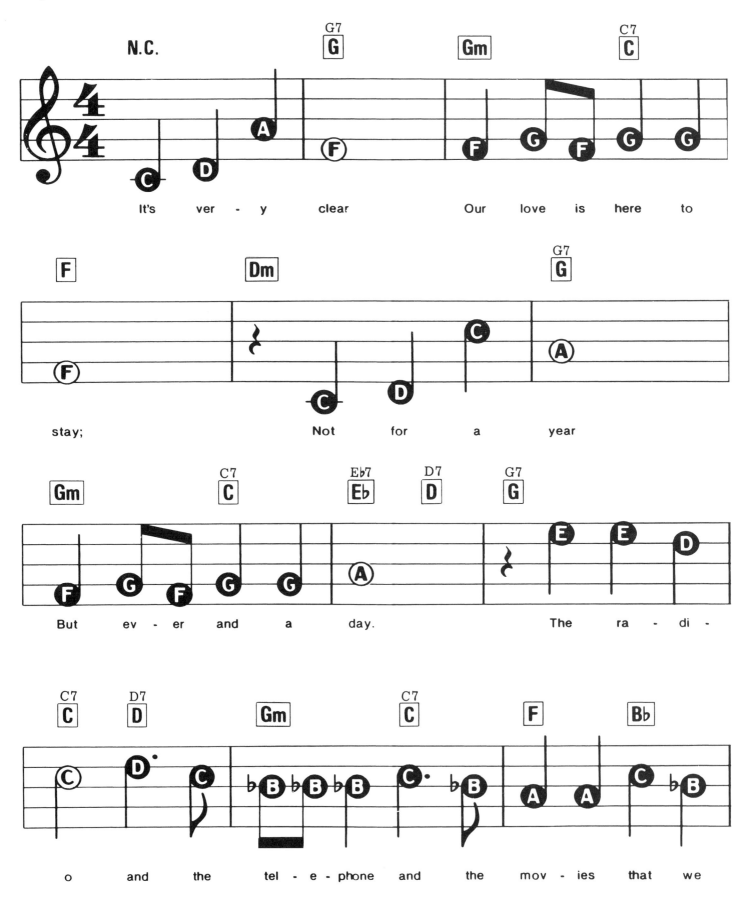

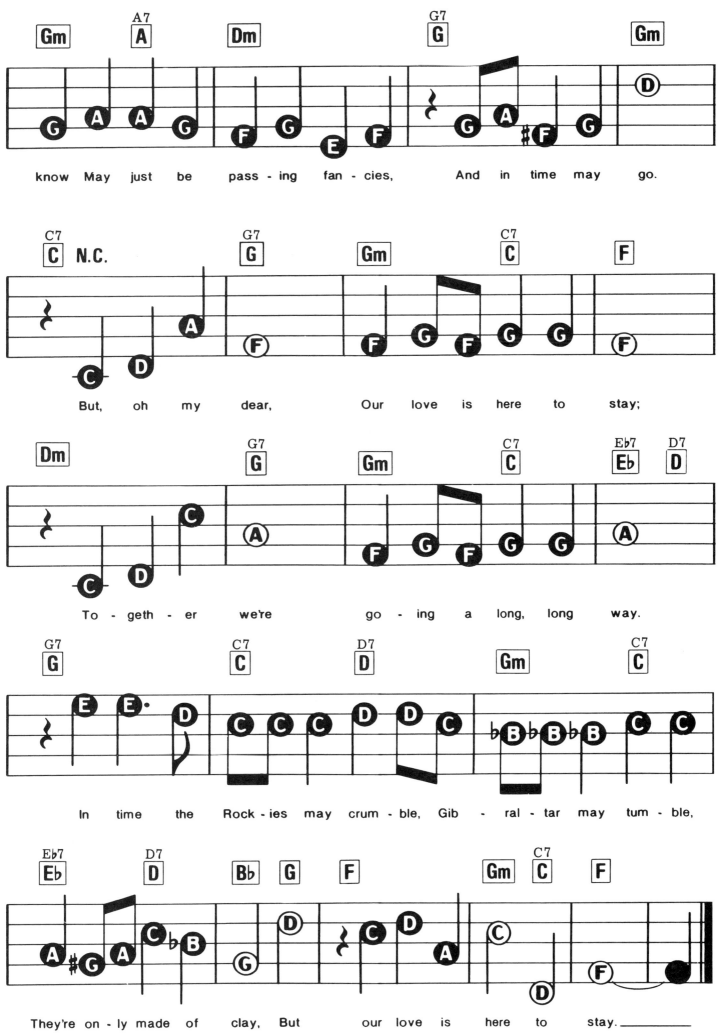

Love Walked In

Registration 9
Rhythm: Swing or Jazz

Music and Lyrics by George Gershwin
and Ira Gershwin

Love walked right in and drove the shad-ows a-

way; Love walked right in and

brought my sun-ni-est day. One

ma-gic mo-ment and my heart seemed to know

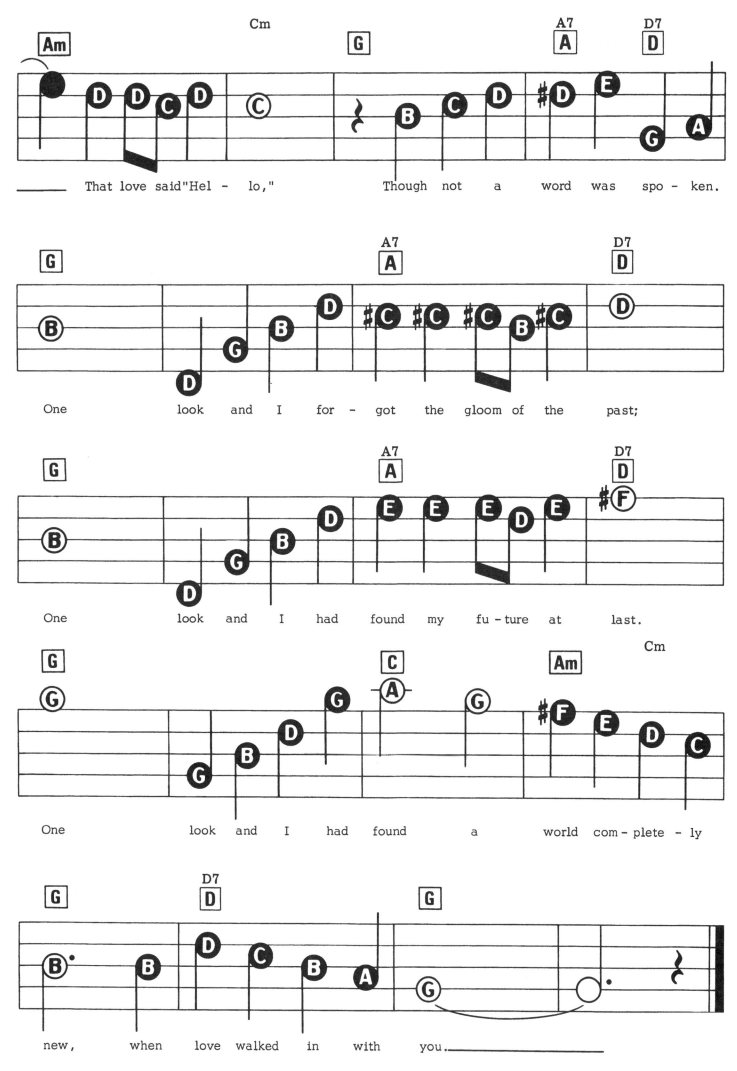

The Man I Love

from LADY BE GOOD
from STRIKE UP THE BAND

Registration 10
Rhythm: Swing or Jazz

Music and Lyrics by George Gershwin
and Ira Gershwin

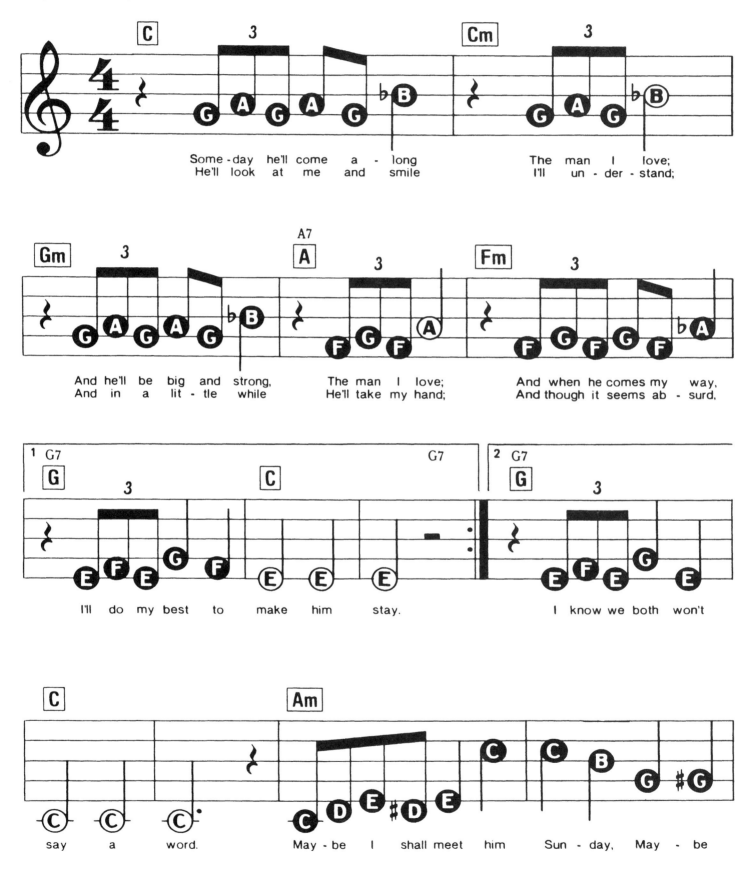

57

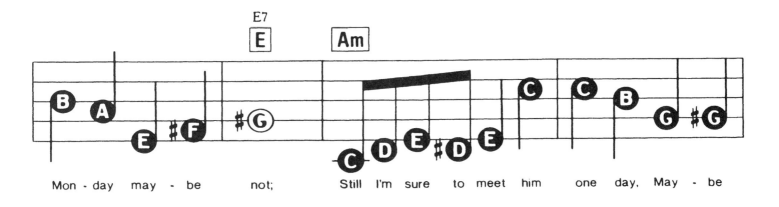

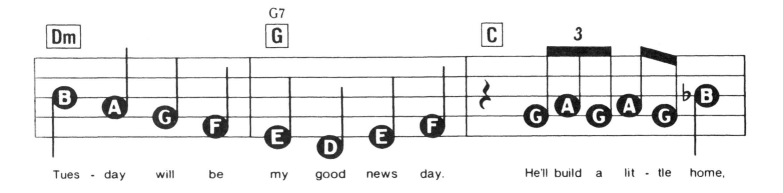

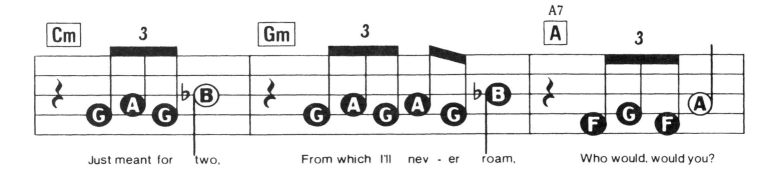

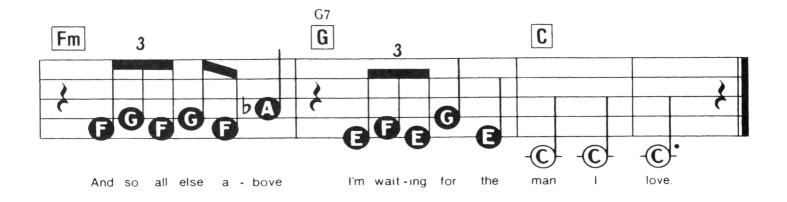

My One and Only

Registration 2
Rhythm: Fox Trot

Words and Music by George Gershwin
and Ira Gershwin

My one and on - ly,

what am I gon - na do if you turn me down, _____

when I'm so cra - zy o - ver you? _____

_____ I'd be so lone - ly,

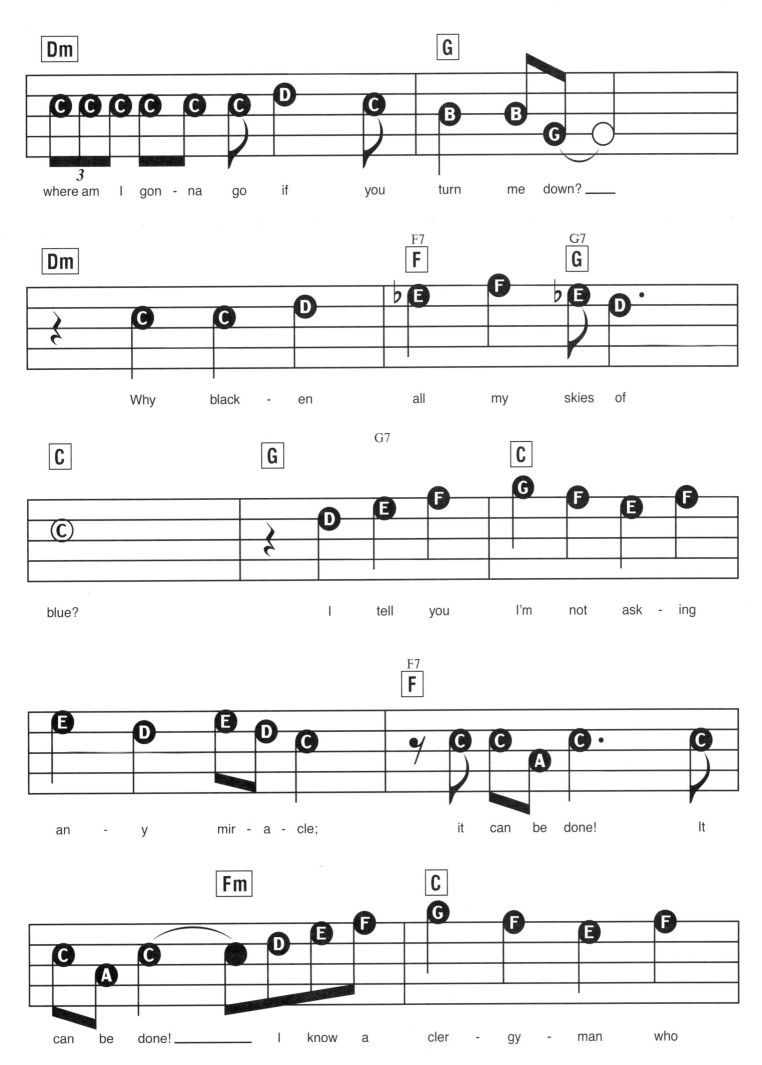

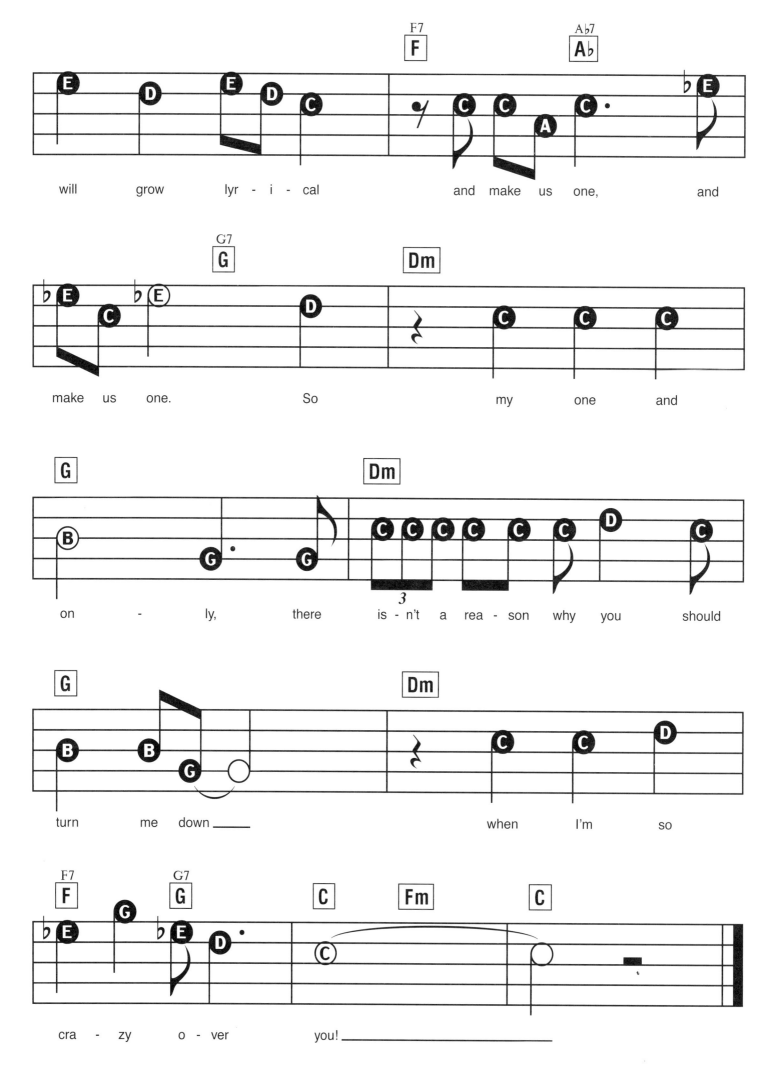

Someone to Watch Over Me

from OH, KAY!

Registration 7
Rhythm: Ballad or Swing

Music and Lyrics by George Gershwin
and Ira Gershwin

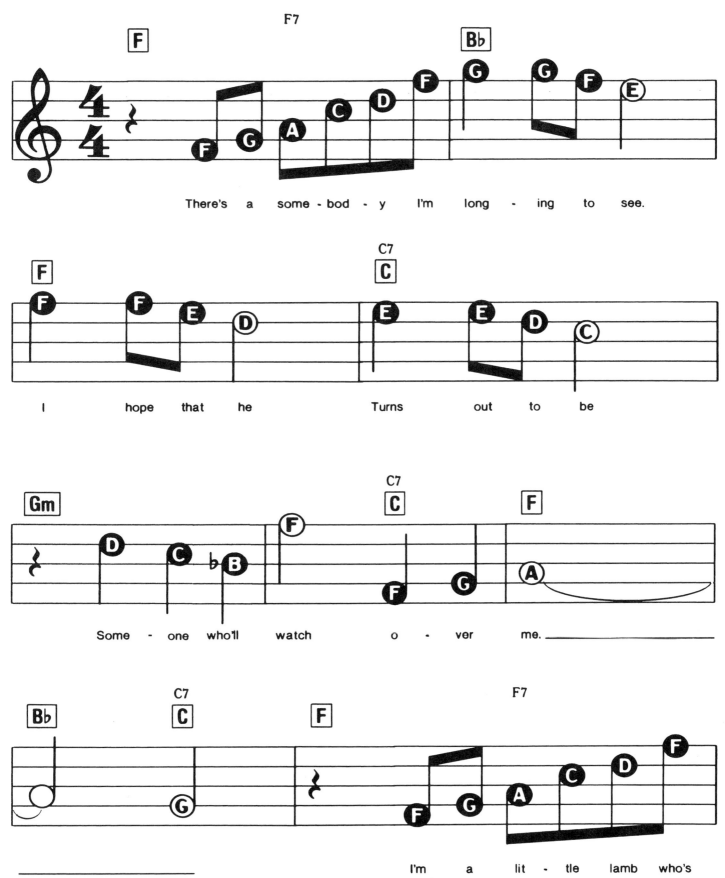

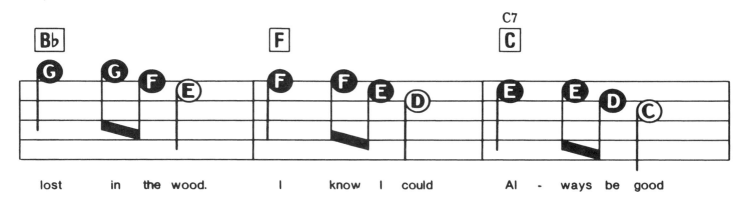

lost   in the wood.   I   know I could   Al - ways be good

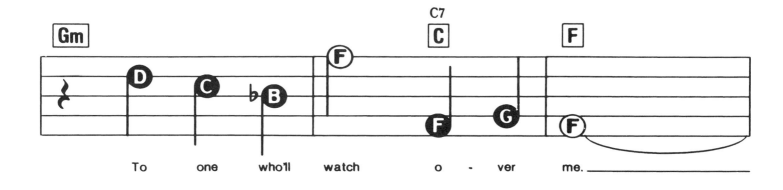

To   one who'll watch   o - ver   me. _____

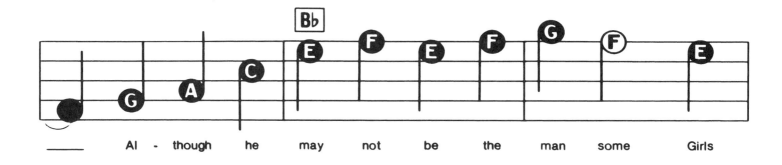

_____ Al - though he may not be the man some Girls

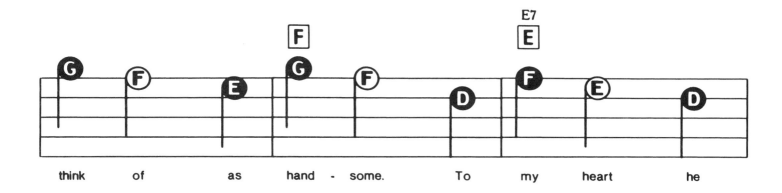

think   of   as hand - some.   To   my heart   he

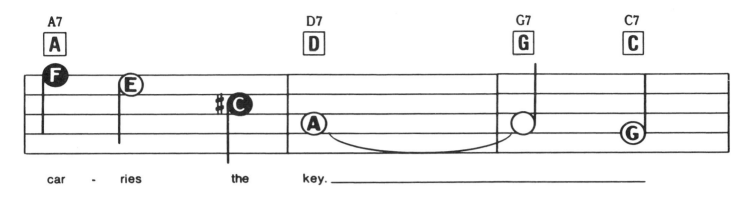

car - ries   the   key. _____

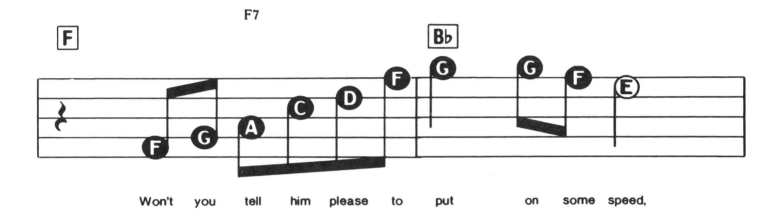

Won't   you   tell   him   please   to   put   on   some   speed,

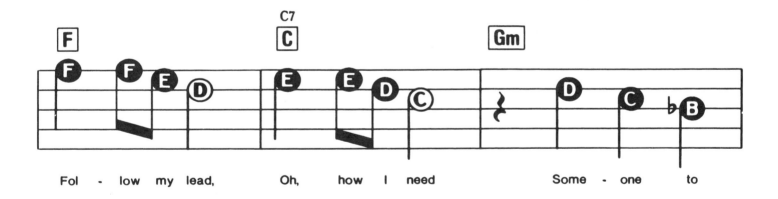

Fol - low   my   lead,   Oh,   how   I   need   Some - one   to

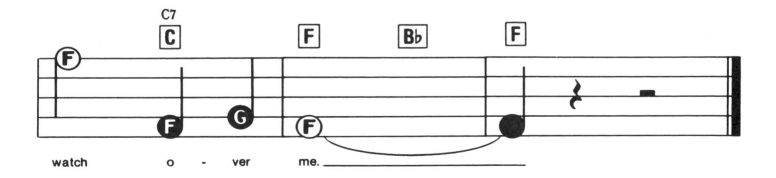

watch   o - ver   me. _____

Nice Work If You Can Get It

from A DAMSEL IN DISTRESS

Registration 7
Rhythm: Swing

Music and Lyrics by George Gershwin
and Ira Gershwin

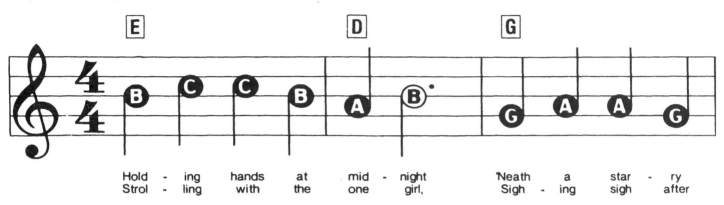

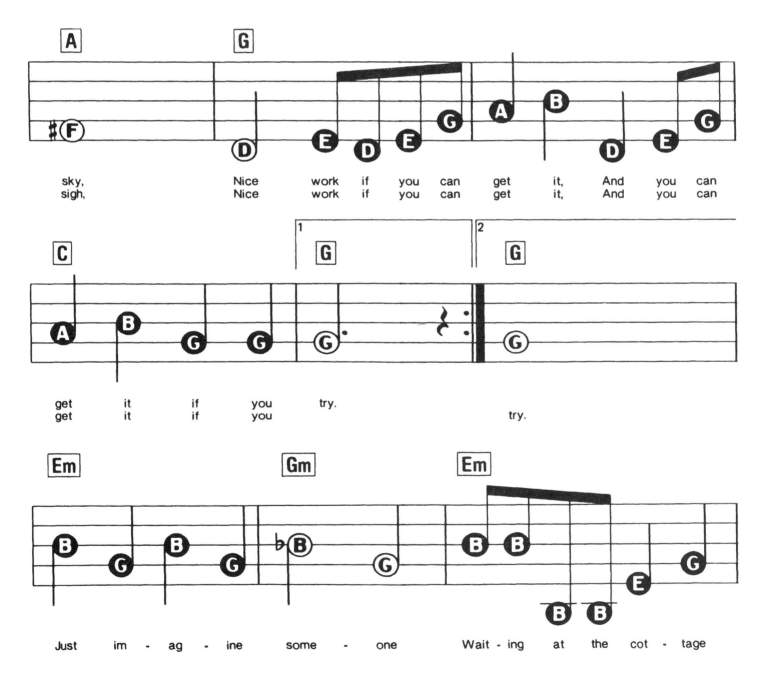

Hold - ing hands at mid - night 'Neath a star - ry
Strol - ling with the one girl, Sigh - ing sigh after

sky, Nice work if you can get it, And you can
sigh, Nice work if you can get it, And you can

get it if you try.
get it if you try.

Just im - ag - ine some - one Wait - ing at the cot - tage

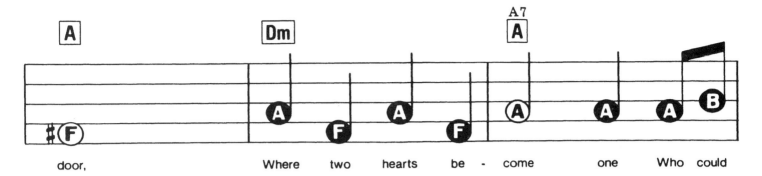

door,　Where　two　hearts　be - come　one　Who could

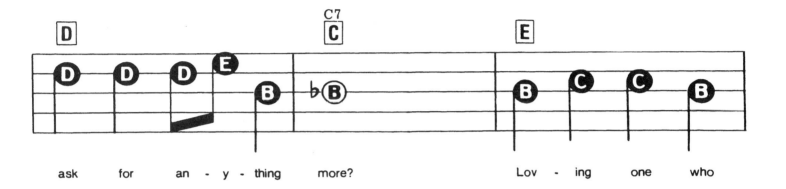

ask　for　an - y - thing　more?　Lov - ing　one　who

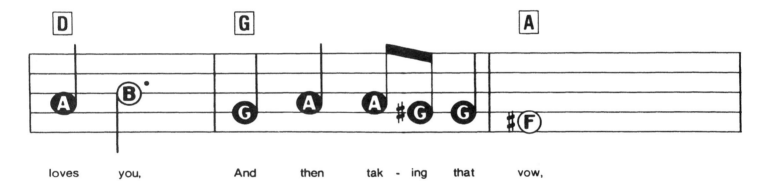

loves　you,　And　then　tak - ing　that　vow,

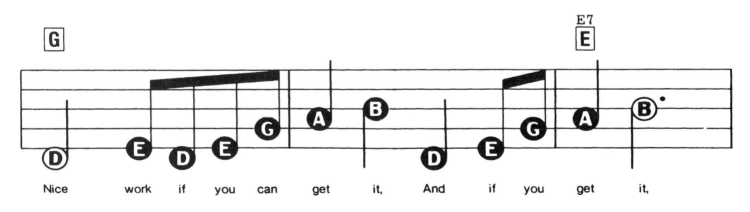

Nice　work　if　you　can　get　it,　And　if　you　get　it,

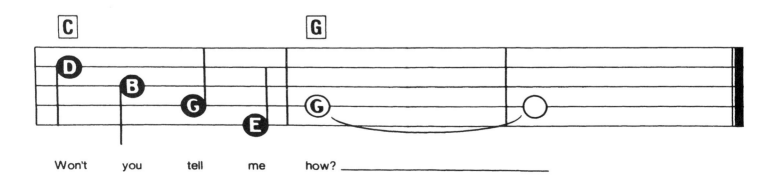

Won't　you　tell　me　how? _____

Of Thee I Sing

Registration 5
Rhythm: Swing or Jazz

Music and Lyrics by George Gershwin
and Ira Gershwin

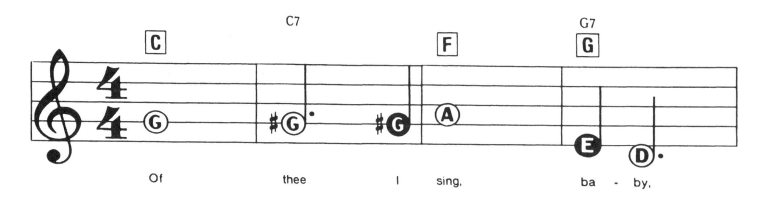

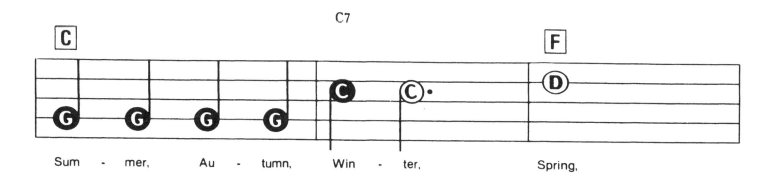

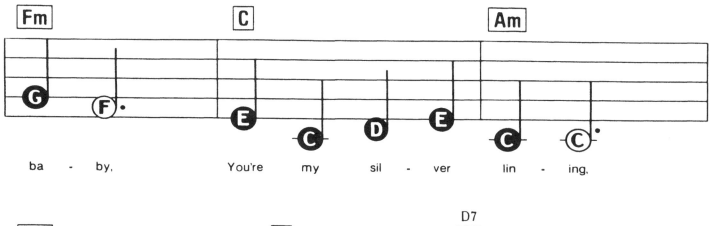

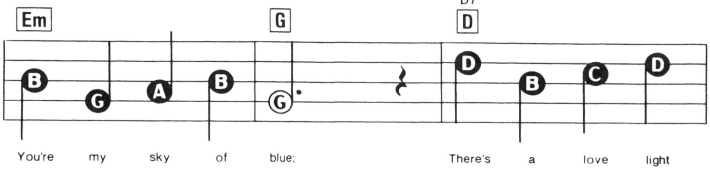

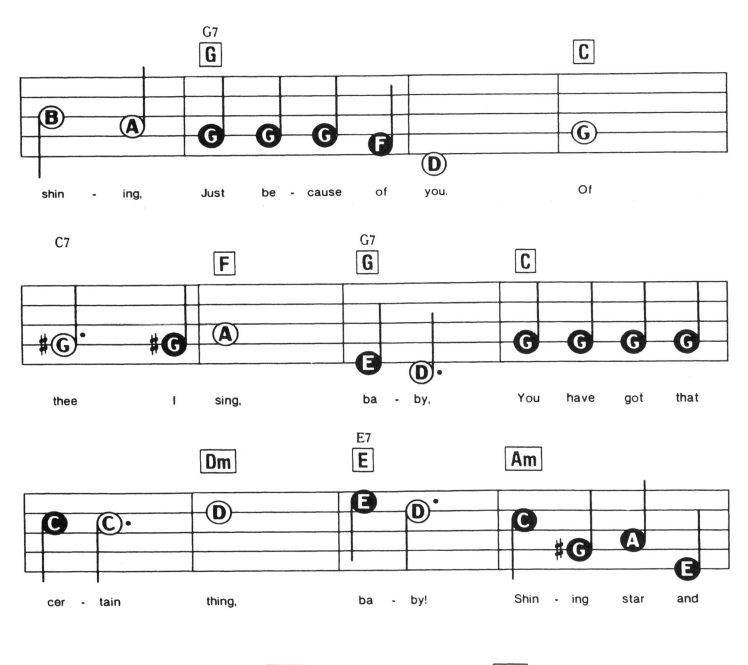

shin - ing, Just be - cause of you. Of

thee I sing, ba - by, You have got that

cer - tain thing, ba - by! Shin - ing star and

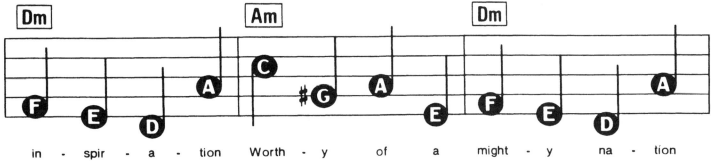

in - spir - a - tion Worth - y of a might - y na - tion

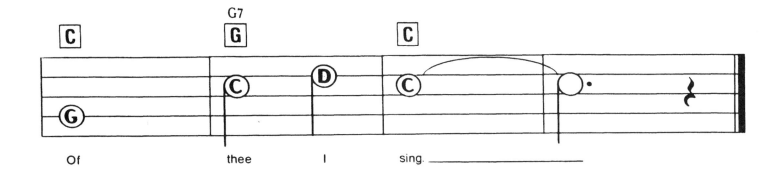

Of thee I sing. _____

Oh, Lady Be Good!

Registration 1
Rhythm: Fox Trot or Swing

Music and Lyrics by George Gershwin
and Ira Gershwin

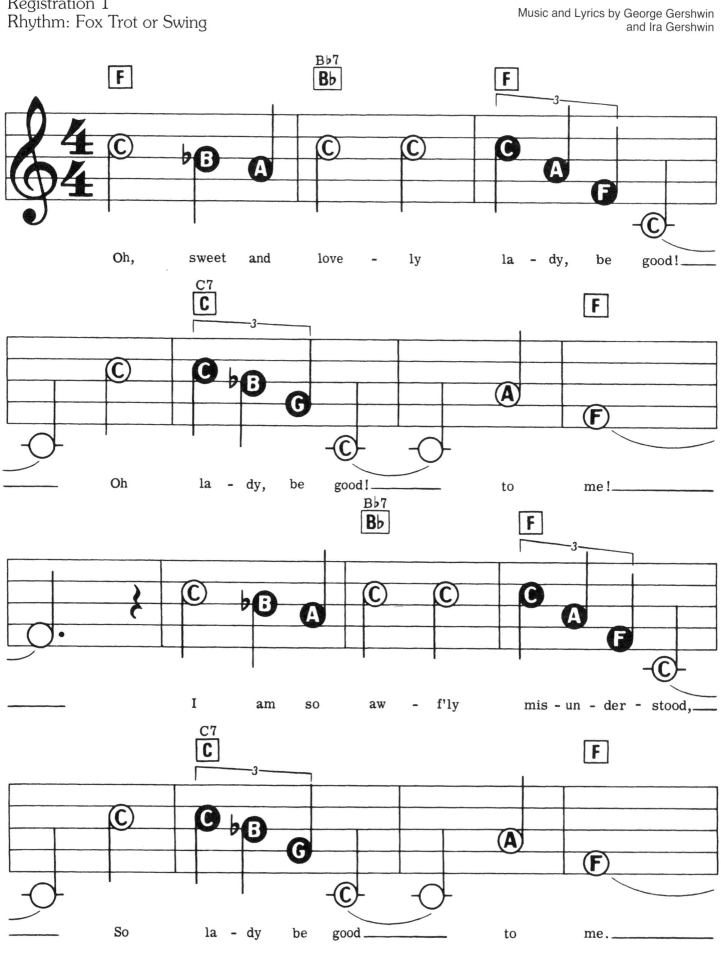

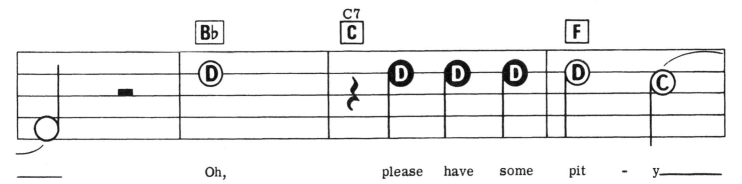

Oh, please have some pit - y ___

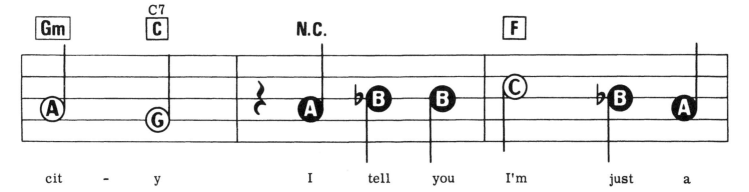

___ I'm all a - lone in this big

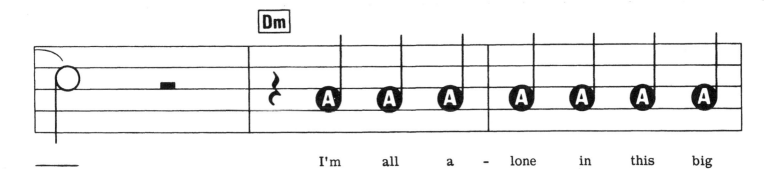

cit - y I tell you I'm just a

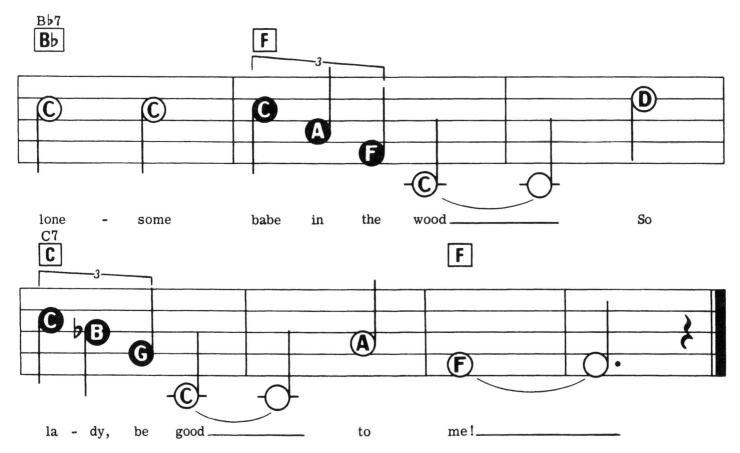

lone - some babe in the wood ___ So

la - dy, be good ___ to me! ___

'S Wonderful
from FUNNY FACE
from AN AMERICAN IN PARIS

Registration 5
Rhythm: Swing or Jazz

Music and Lyrics by George Gershwin
and Ira Gershwin

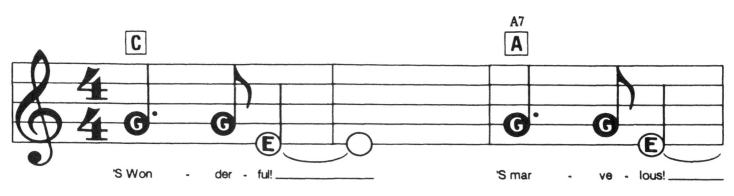

'S Won - der - ful! _____ 'S mar - ve - lous! _____

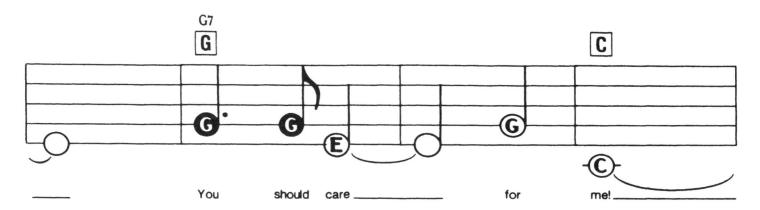

____ You should care _____ for me! _____

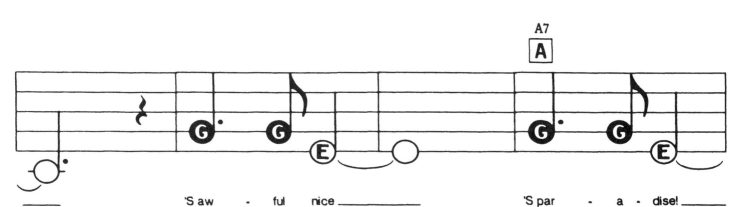

____ 'S aw - ful nice _____ 'S par - a - dise! _____

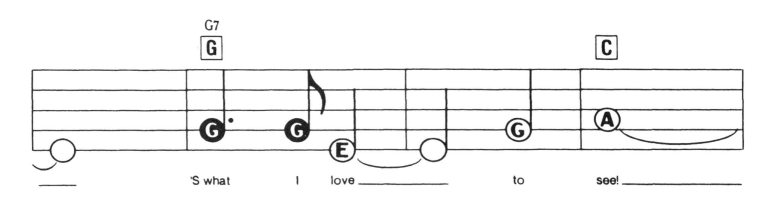

____ 'S what I love _____ to see! _____

71

Shall We Dance?

Registration 7
Rhythm: Fox Trot

Words and Music by George Gershwin
and Ira Gershwin

Shall we dance, or keep on

mop - ing? Shall we dance, and walk on

air? Shall we give in to des -

pair, or shall we dance with nev - er a

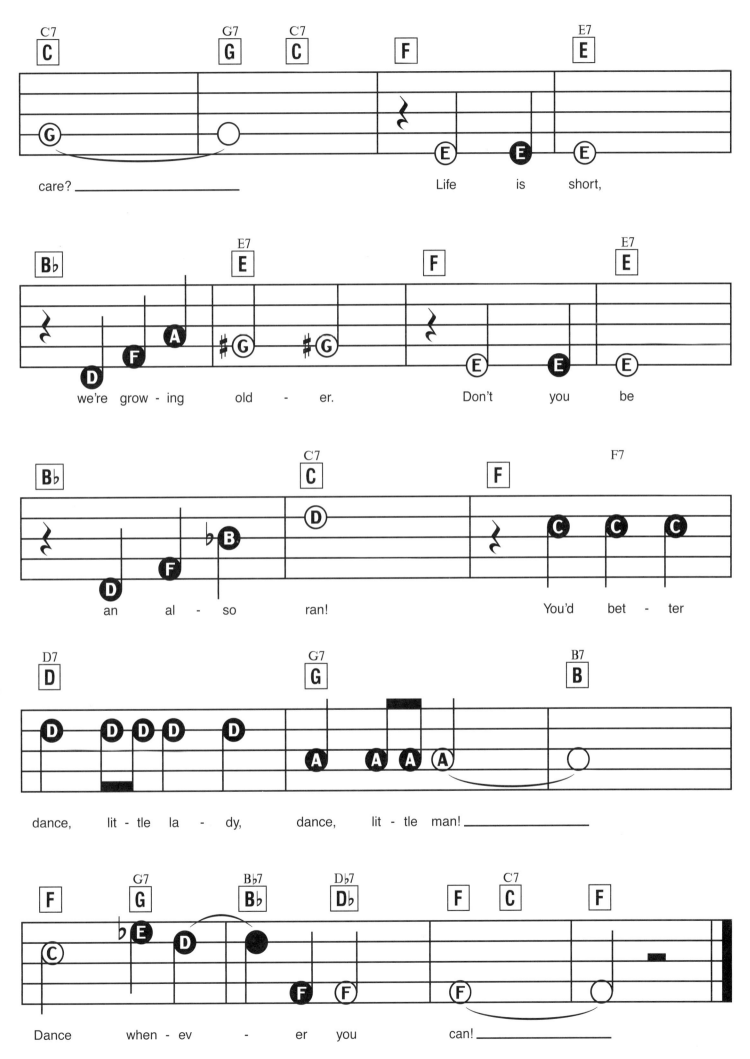

Somebody Loves Me
from GEORGE WHITE'S SCANDALS OF 1924

Registration 4
Rhythm: Fox Trot or Swing

Music by George Gershwin
Lyrics by B.G. DeSylva and Ballard MacDonald
French Version by Emelia Renaud

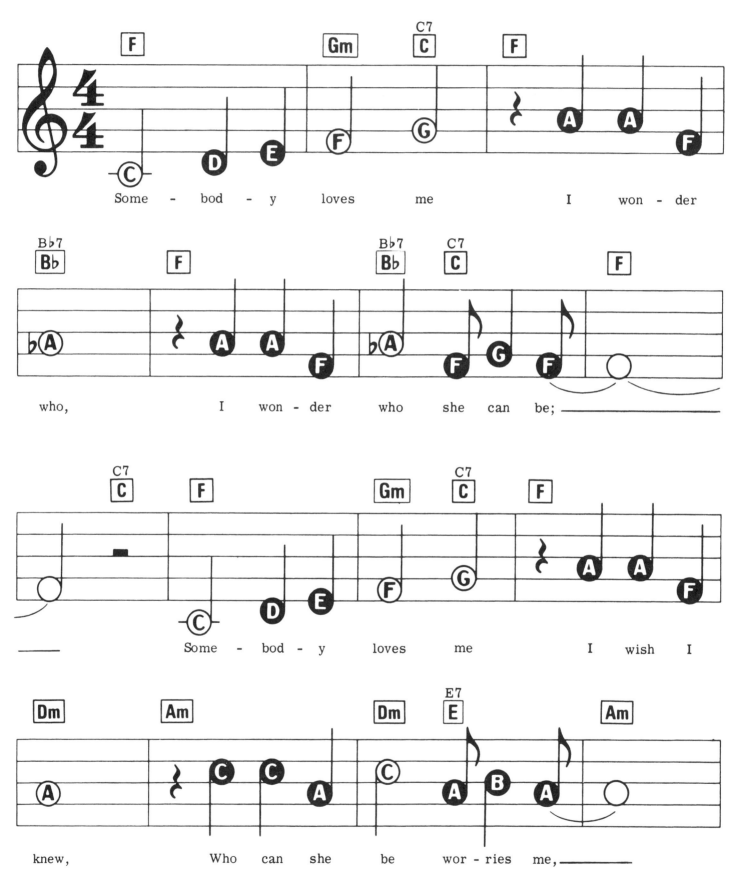

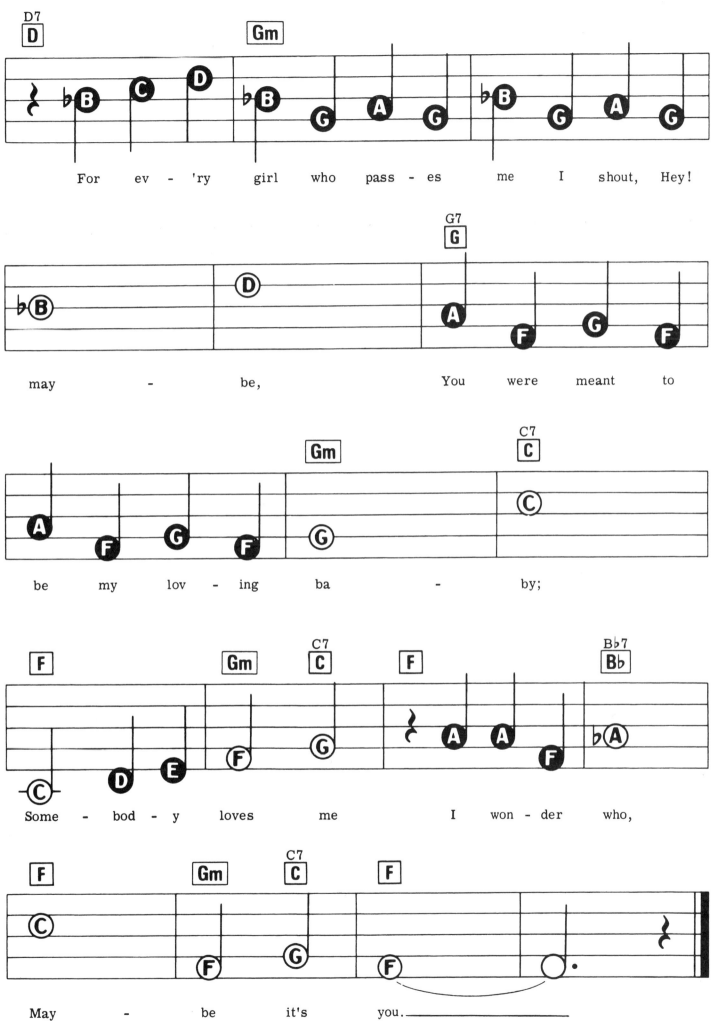

Strike Up the Band
from STRIKE UP THE BAND

Registration 4
Rhythm: March or Polka

Music and Lyrics by George Gershwin
and Ira Gershwin

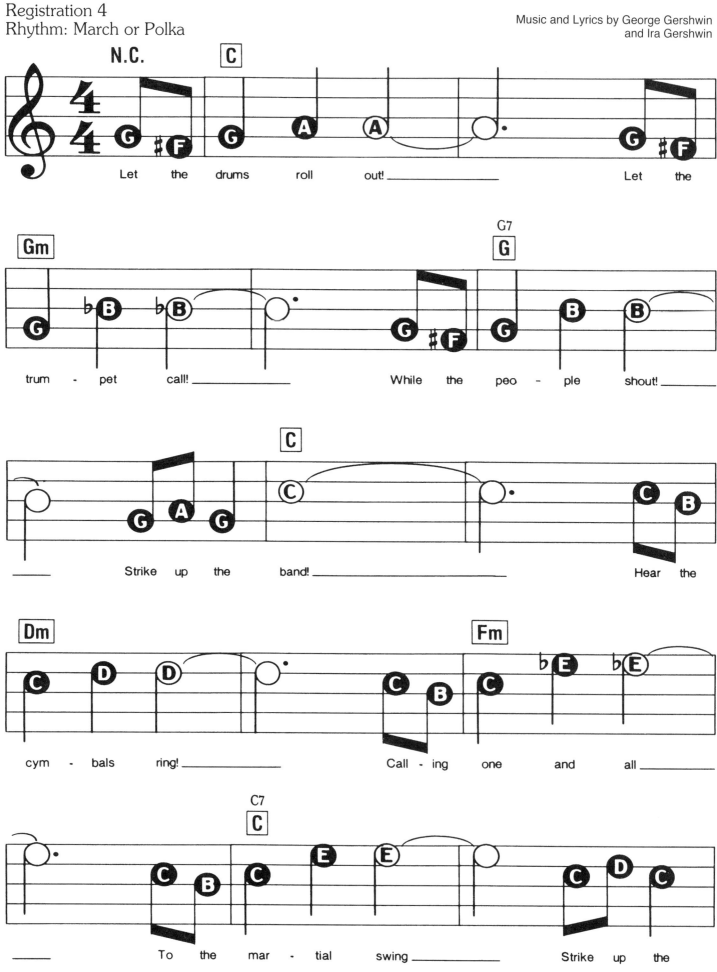

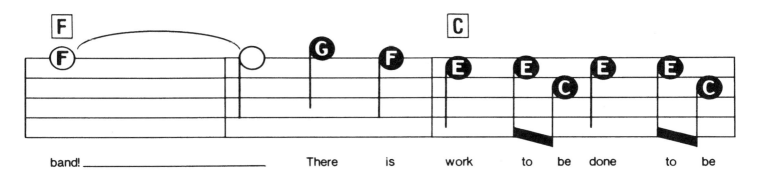

band! _____ There is work to be done to be

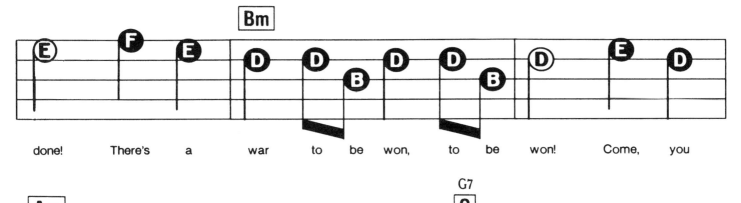

done! There's a war to be won, to be won! Come, you

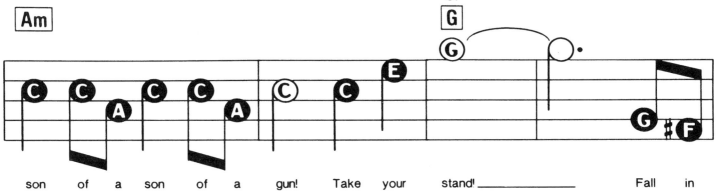

son of a son of a gun! Take your stand! _____ Fall in

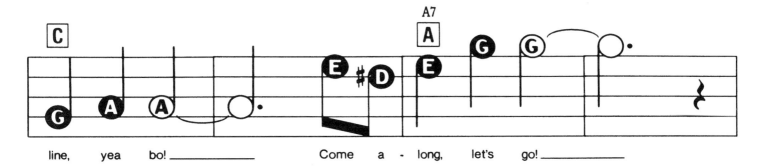

line, yea bo! _____ Come a - long, let's go! _____

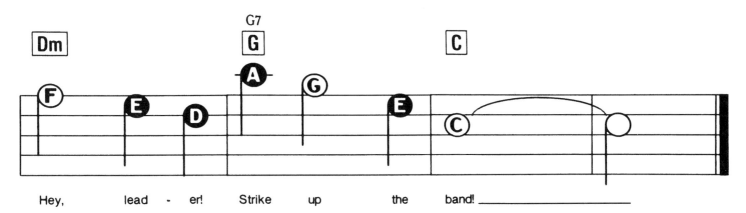

Hey, lead - er! Strike up the band! _____

Summertime
from PORGY AND BESS®

Registration 10
Rhythm: Ballad or Blues

Music and Lyrics by George Gershwin,
Du Bose and Dorothy Heyward
and Ira Gershwin

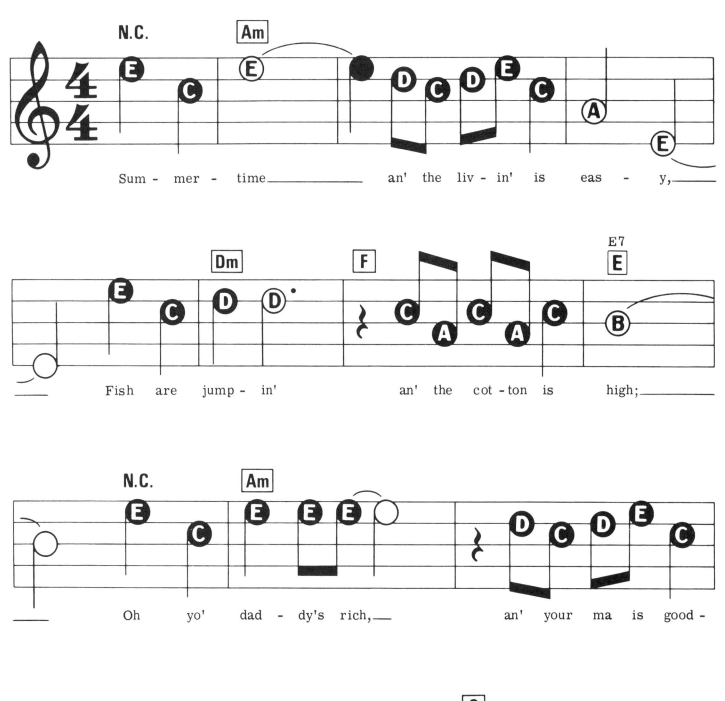

Sum - mer - time_____ an' the liv - in' is eas - y,_____

Fish are jump - in'_____ an' the cot - ton is high;_____

Oh yo' dad - dy's rich,_____ an' your ma is good -

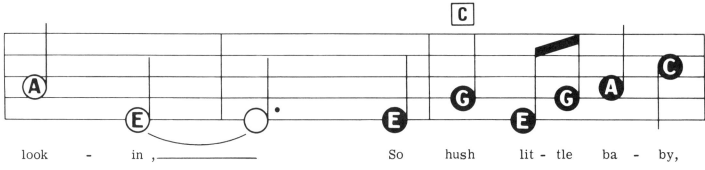

look - in ,_____ So hush lit - tle ba - by,

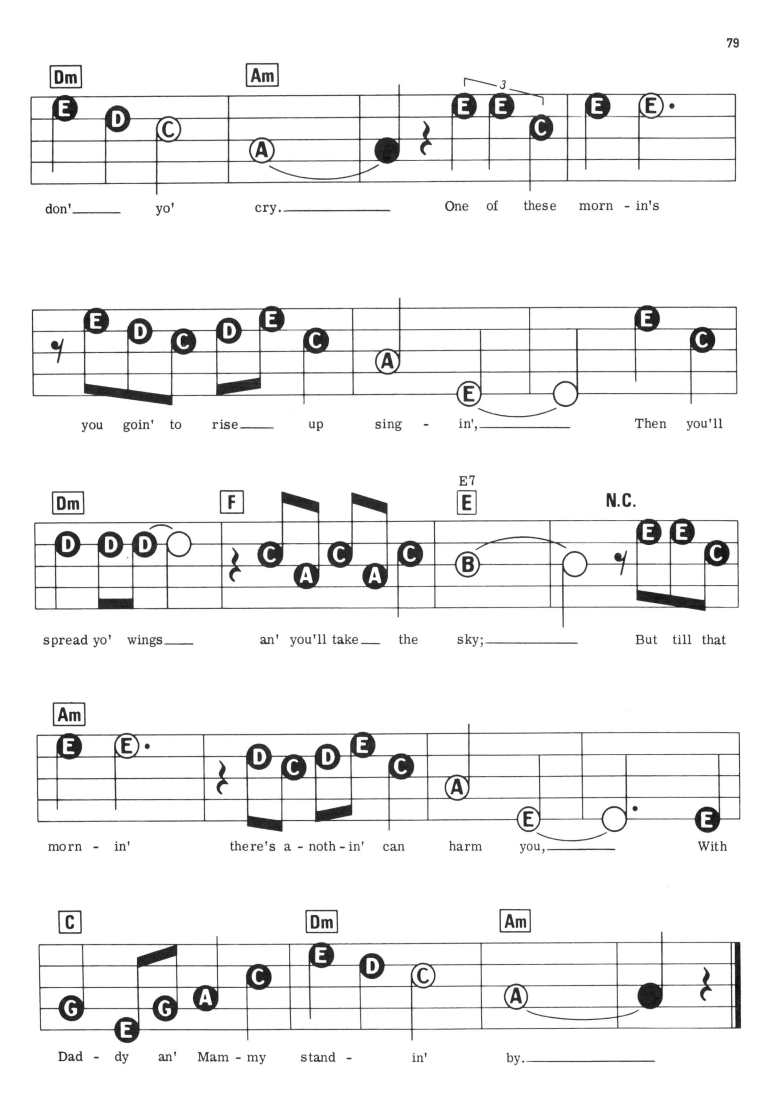

Swanee

Registration 9
Rhythm: Fox Trot or Swing

Words by Irving Caesar
Music by George Gershwin

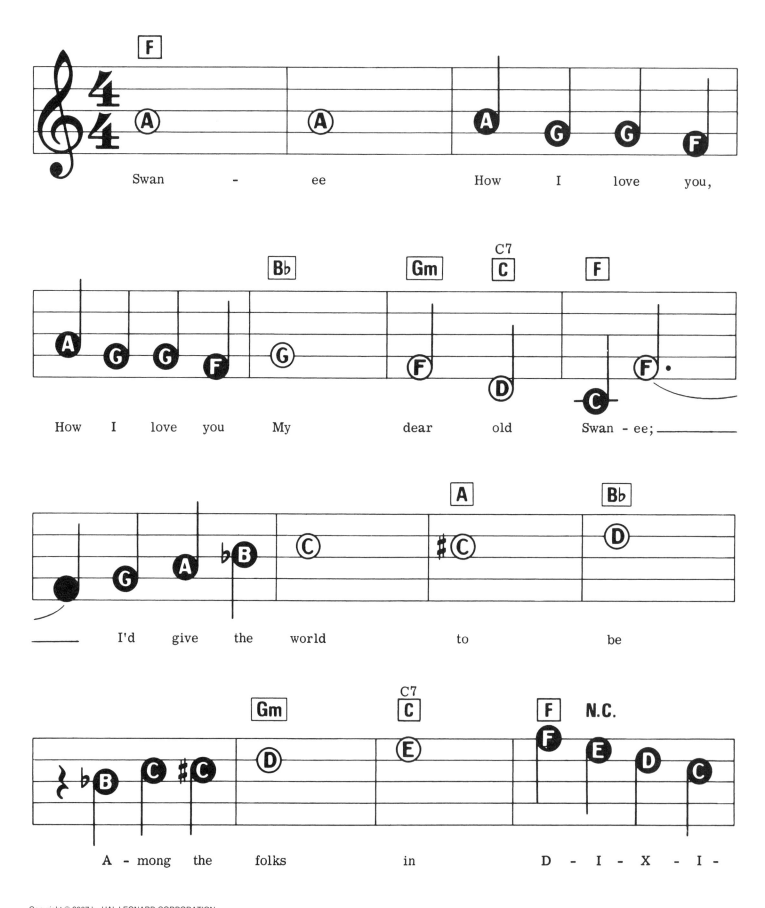

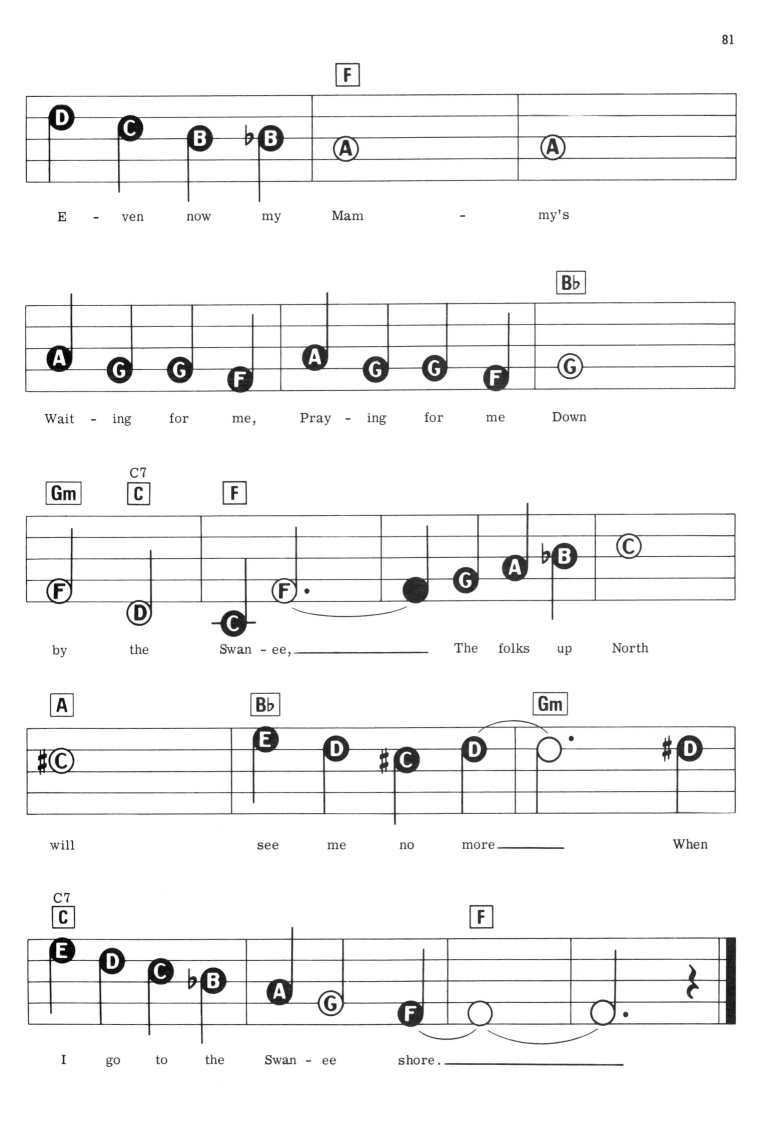

They Can't Take That Away from Me

from THE BARKLEYS OF BROADWAY
from SHALL WE DANCE

Registration 1
Rhythm: Ballad or Fox Trot

Music and Lyrics by George Gershwin
and Ira Gershwin

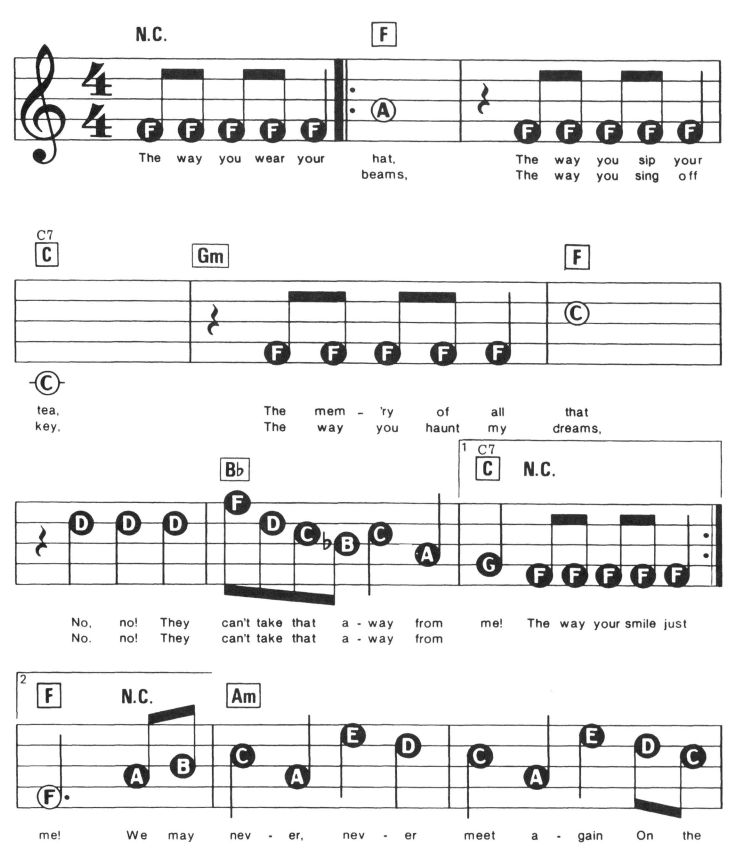

83

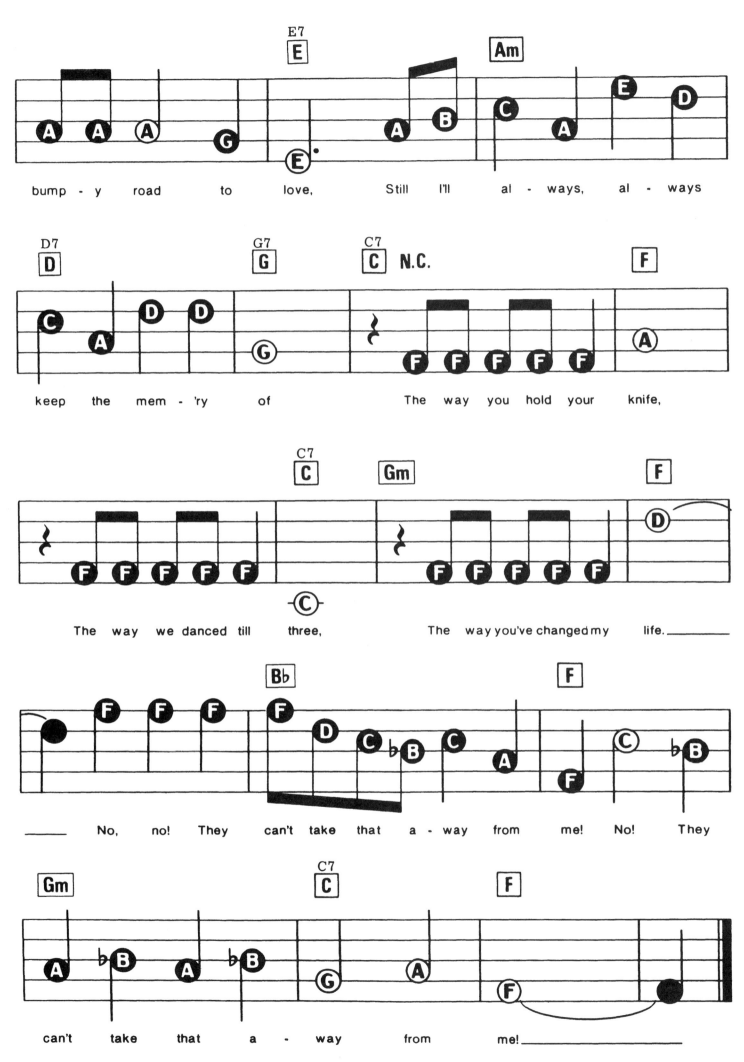

They All Laughed

Registration 9
Rhythm: Swing

Music and Lyrics by George Gershwin
and Ira Gershwin

They all laughed at Chris - to - pher Co - lum - bus
They all laughed at Rock - e - fel - ler Cen - ter

When he said the World was round.
Now they're fight - ing to get in.

They all laughed when
They all laughed at

Ed - i - son re - cord - ed sound. _____
Whit - ney and his cot - ton gin. _____

They all laughed at
They all laughed at

Wil - bur and his broth - er,
Ful - ton and his steam - boat

When they said that man could fly.
Her - shey and his choc' - late bar.

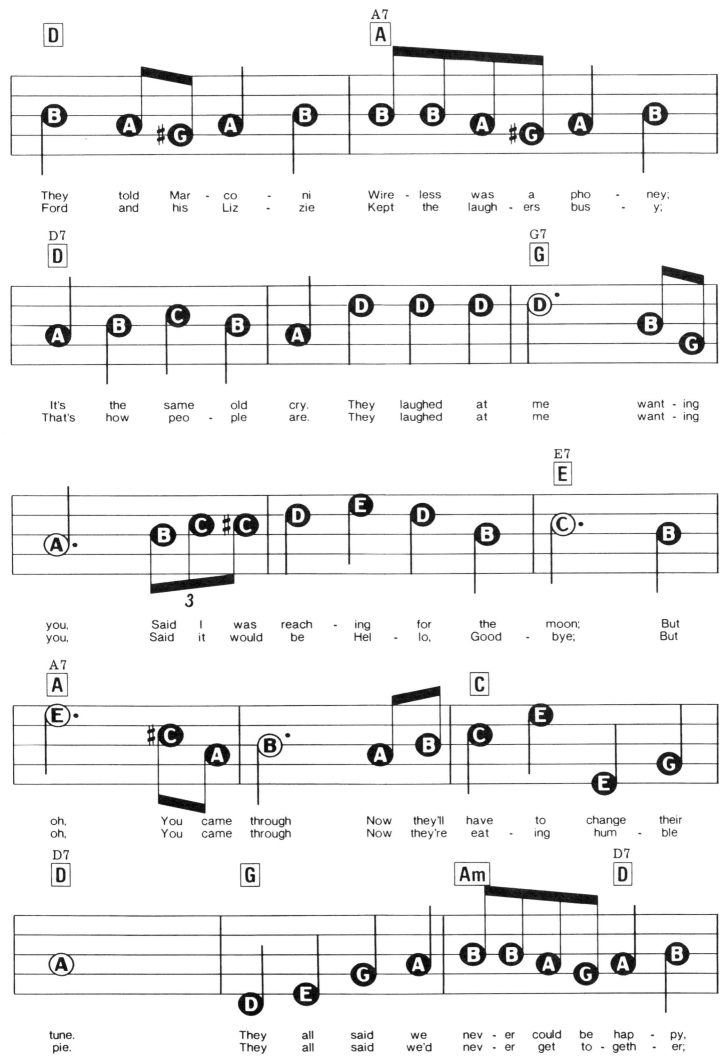

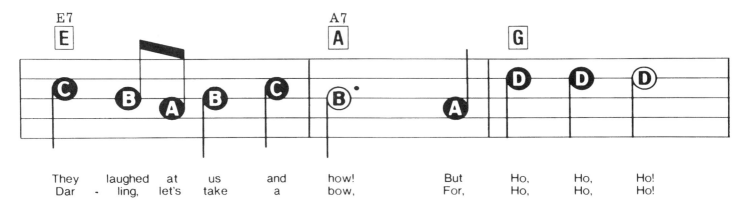

They laughed at us and how! But Ho, Ho, Ho!
Dar - ling, let's take a bow, For, Ho, Ho, Ho!

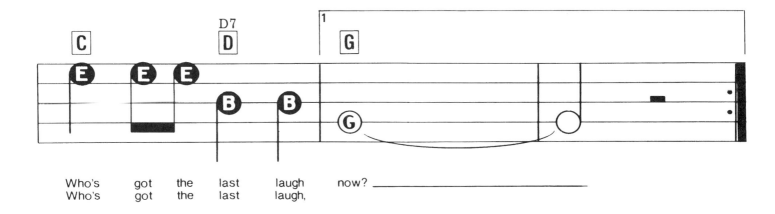

Who's got the last laugh now? _____
Who's got the last laugh,

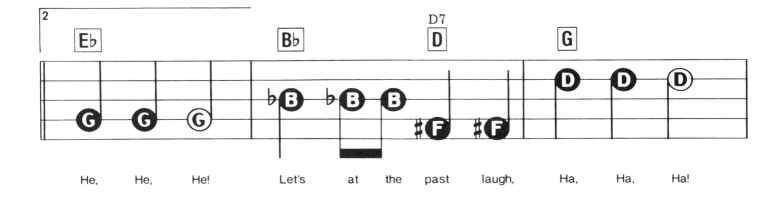

He, He, He! Let's at the past laugh, Ha, Ha, Ha!

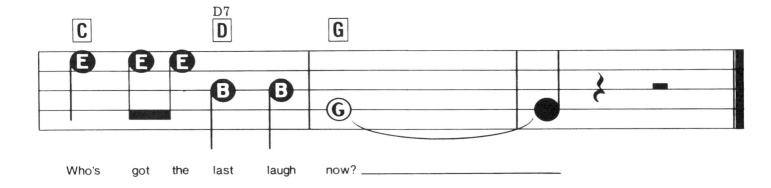

Who's got the last laugh now? _____

Registration
Guide

- Match the Registration number on the song to the corresponding numbered category below. Select and activate an instrumental sound available on your instrument.

- Choose an automatic rhythm appropriate to the mood and style of the song. (Consult your Owner's Guide for proper operation of automatic rhythm features.)

- Adjust the tempo and volume controls to comfortable settings.

Registration

1	Mellow	Flutes, Clarinet, Oboe, Flugel Horn, Trombone, French Horn, Organ Flutes
2	Ensemble	Brass Section, Sax Section, Wind Ensemble, Full Organ, Theater Organ
3	Strings	Violin, Viola, Cello, Fiddle, String Ensemble, Pizzicato, Organ Strings
4	Guitars	Acoustic/Electric Guitars, Banjo, Mandolin, Dulcimer, Ukulele, Hawaiian Guitar
5	Mallets	Vibraphone, Marimba, Xylophone, Steel Drums, Bells, Celesta, Chimes
6	Liturgical	Pipe Organ, Hand Bells, Vocal Ensemble, Choir, Organ Flutes
7	Bright	Saxophones, Trumpet, Mute Trumpet, Synth Leads, Jazz/Gospel Organs
8	Piano	Piano, Electric Piano, Honky Tonk Piano, Harpsichord, Clavi
9	Novelty	Melodic Percussion, Wah Trumpet, Synth, Whistle, Kazoo, Perc. Organ
10	Bellows	Accordion, French Accordion, Mussette, Harmonica, Pump Organ, Bagpipes

FOR ORGANS, PIANOS & ELECTRONIC KEYBOARDS

E-Z PLAY® TODAY PUBLICATIONS

The E-Z Play® Today songbook series is the shortest distance between beginning music a playing fun! Check out this list of highlights and visit www.halleonard.com for a compl listing of all volumes and songlists.

00102278	1. Favorite Songs with 3 Chords	$7.95
00100374	2. Country Sound	$8.95
00100167	3. Contemporary Disney	$16.99
00100382	4. Dance Band Greats	$7.95
00100305	5. All-Time Standards	$7.99
00100428	6. Songs of The Beatles	$10.99
00100442	7. Hits from Musicals	$7.95
00100490	8. Patriotic Songs	$7.95
00100355	9. Christmas Time	$7.95
00100435	10. Hawaiian Songs	$7.95
00100248	13. Three-Chord Country Songs	$12.95
00100300	14. All-Time Requests	$8.99
00100370	15. Country Pickin's	$7.95
00100335	16. Broadway's Best	$7.95
00100362	18. Classical Portraits	$7.99
00102277	20. Hymns	$7.95
00100570	22. Sacred Sounds	$7.95
00100214	23. Essential Songs – The 1920s	$16.95
00100206	24. Essential Songs – The 1930s	$16.95
00100207	25. Essential Songs – The 1940s	$16.95
14041364	26. Bob Dylan	$12.99
00001236	27. 60 of the World's Easiest to Play Songs with 3 Chords	$8.95
00101598	28. Fifty Classical Themes	$9.95
00100135	29. Love Songs	$7.95
00100030	30. Country Connection	$8.95
00001289	32. Sing-Along Favorites	$7.95
00100253	34. Inspirational Ballads	$10.95
00100254	35. Frank Sinatra – Romance	$8.95
00100122	36. Good Ol' Songs	$10.95
00100410	37. Favorite Latin Songs	$7.95
00100032	38. Songs of the '90s	$12.95
00100425	41. Songs of Gershwin, Porter & Rodgers	$7.95
00100123	42. Baby Boomers Songbook	$9.95
00100576	43. Sing-along Requests	$8.95
00102135	44. Best of Willie Nelson	$8.95
00100460	45. Love Ballads	$8.99
00100343	48. Gospel Songs of Johnny Cash	$7.95
00100043	49. Elvis, Elvis, Elvis	$9.95
00102114	50. Best of Patsy Cline	$9.95
00100208	51. Essential Songs – The 1950s	$17.95
00100209	52. Essential Songs – The 1960s	$17.95
00100210	53. Essential Songs – The 1970s	$19.95
00100211	54. Essential Songs – The 1980s	$19.95
00100342	55. Johnny Cash	$9.99
00100118	57. More of the Best Songs Ever	$17.99
00100285	58. Four-Chord Songs	$10.99
00100353	59. Christmas Songs	$8.95
00100304	60. Songs for All Occasions	$16.99
00102314	61. Jazz Standards	$10.95
00100409	62. Favorite Hymns	$6.95
00100360	63. Classical Music (Spanish/English)	$6.95
00100223	64. Wicked	$9.95
00100217	65. Hymns with 3 Chords	$7.95
00102312	66. Torch Songs	$14.95
00100218	67. Music from the Motion Picture Ray	$8.95
00100449	69. It's Gospel	$7.95
00100432	70. Gospel Greats	$7.95
00100117	72. Canciones Románticas	$6.95
00100121	73. Movie Love Songs	$7.95
00100568	75. Sacred Moments	$6.95
00100572	76. The Sound of Music	$8.95
00100489	77. My Fair Lady	$6.95
00100424	81. Frankie Yankovic – Polkas & Waltzes	$7.95
00100579	86. Songs from Musicals	$7.95
00100286	87. 50 Worship Standards	$14.99
00100287	88. Glee	$9.99
00100577	89. Songs for Children	$7.95
00290104	90. Elton John Anthology	$16.99
00100034	91. 30 Songs for a Better World	$8.95
00100288	92. Michael Bublé – Crazy Love	$10.99
00100036	93. Country Hits	$10.95
00100139	94. Jim Croce – Greatest Hits	$8.95
00100219	95. The Phantom of the Opera (Movie)	$10.95
00100263	96. Mamma Mia – Movie Soundtrack	$7.99
00102317	97. Elvis Presley – Songs of Inspiration	$12.99
00100125	99. Children's Christmas Songs	$7.95
00100602	100. Winter Wonderland	$8.95

00001309	102. Carols of Christmas	$7.99
00100127	103. Greatest Songs of the Last Century	$16.95
00100256	107. The Best Praise & Worship Songs Ever	$16.99
00100363	108. Classical Themes (English/Spanish)	$6.95
00102232	109. Motown's Greatest Hits	$12.95
00101566	110. Neil Diamond Collection	$14.99
00100119	111. Season's Greetings	$14.95
00101498	112. Best of The Beatles	$19.95
00100134	113. Country Gospel USA	$10.95
00101612	115. The Greatest Waltzes	$9.95
00100257	116. Amy Grant – Greatest Hits	$9.95
00100136	118. 100 Kids' Songs	$12.95
00101990	119. 57 Super Hits	$12.95
00100433	120. Gospel of Bill & Gloria Gaither	$14.95
00100333	121. Boogies, Blues and Rags	$7.95
00100146	122. Songs for Praise & Worship	$8.95
00100001	125. Great Big Book of Children's Songs	$12.95
00101563	127. John Denver's Greatest Hits	$9.95
00100037	129. The Groovy Years	$12.95
00102318	131. Doo-Wop Songbook	$10.95
00100306	133. Carole King	$9.99
00100171	135. All Around the U.S.A.	$10.95
00001256	136. Christmas Is for Kids	$8.99
00100144	137. Children's Movie Hits	$7.95
00100038	138. Nostalgia Collection	$14.95
00100289	139. Crooners	$19.99
00101956	140. Best of George Strait	$12.95
00100290	141. All Time Latin Favorites	$7.95
00100314	142. Classic Jazz	$14.99
00101946	143. The Songs of Paul McCartney	$8.99
00100013	144. All Time TV Favorites	$17.95
00100597	146. Hank Williams – His Best	$7.95
00100003	149. Movie Musical Memories	$10.95
00101548	150. Best Big Band Songs Ever	$16.95
00100152	151. Beach Boys – Greatest Hits	$8.95
00101592	152. Fiddler on the Roof	$9.99
00101549	155. Best of Billy Joel	$10.99
00100033	156. Best of Rodgers & Hart	$7.95
00001264	157. Easy Favorites	$7.99
00100315	160. The Grammy Awards Record of the Year 1958-2010	$16.99
00100293	161. Henry Mancini	$9.99
00100049	162. Lounge Music	$10.95
00100295	163. The Very Best of the Rat Pack	$12.99
00101530	164. Best Christmas Songbook	$9.95
00101895	165. Rodgers & Hammerstein Songbook	$9.95
00100140	167. Christian Children's Songbook	$10.95
00100148	169. A Charlie Brown Christmas™	$8.99
00101900	170. Kenny Rogers – Greatest Hits	$9.95
00101537	171. Best of Elton John	$7.95
00100149	176. Charlie Brown Collection™	$7.99
00102325	179. Love Songs of The Beatles	$10.99
00101610	181. Great American Country Songbook	$12.95
00001246	182. Amazing Grace	$12.95
00450133	183. West Side Story	$9.99
00100151	185. Carpenters	$10.99
00101606	186. 40 Pop & Rock Song Classics	$12.95
00100155	187. Ultimate Christmas	$17.95
00102276	189. Irish Favorites	$7.95
00101939	190. 17 Super Christmas Hits	$8.95
00100053	191. Jazz Love Songs	$8.95
00101998	192. 65 Standard Hits	$15.95
00101941	194. 67 Standard Hits	$16.95
00101609	196. Best of George Gershwin	$9.99
00100057	198. Songs in 3/4 Time	$9.95
00100453	199. Jumbo Songbook	$19.95
00101539	200. Best Songs Ever	$19.95
00101540	202. Best Country Songs Ever	$17.95
00101541	203. Best Broadway Songs Ever	$17.99
00101542	204. Best Easy Listening Songs Ever	$17.95
00101543	205. Best Love Songs Ever	$17.95
00100058	208. Easy Listening Favorites	$7.95
00100059	210. '60s Pop Rock Hits	$12.95
00101546	213. Disney Classics	$14.95
00101533	215. Best Christmas Songs Ever	$19.95
00100156	219. Christmas Songs with 3 Chords	$8.99
00102080	225. Lawrence Welk Songbook	$9.95
00101931	228. Songs of the '20s	$13.95

00101932	229. Songs of the '30s	$13.
00101933	230. Songs of the '40s	$14.
00101934	231. Songs of the '50s	$14.
00101935	232. Songs of the '60s	$14.
00101936	233. Songs of the '70s	$14.
00101581	235. Elvis Presley Anthology	$15.
00290059	238. 25 Top Christmas Songs	$9.
00290170	239. Big Book of Children's Songs	$14.
00290120	240. Frank Sinatra	$14.
00100158	243. Oldies! Oldies! Oldies!	$10.
00290242	244. Songs of the '80s	$14.
00100041	245. Best of Simon & Garfunkel	$8.
00100269	247. Essential Songs – Broadway	$17.
00100296	248. The Love Songs of Elton John	$12.
00100175	249. Elvis – 30 #1 Hits	$9.
00102113	251. Phantom of the Opera (Broadway)	$14.
00100301	255. Four-Chord Hymns	$8.
00100203	256. Very Best of Lionel Richie	$8.
00100302	258. Four-Chord Worship	$9.
00100178	259. Norah Jones – Come Away with Me	$9.
00102306	261. Best of Andrew Lloyd Webber	$12.
00100063	266. Latin Hits	$7.
00100062	269. Love That Latin Beat	$7.
00100179	270. Christian Christmas Songbook	$14.
00101425	272. ABBA Gold – Greatest Hits	$7.
00102248	275. Classical Hits – Bach, Beethoven & Brahms	$6.
00100186	277. Stevie Wonder – Greatest Hits	$9.
00100237	280. Dolly Parton	$9.
00100068	283. Best Jazz Standards Ever	$15.
00100244	287. Josh Groban	$10.
00100022	288. Sing-a-Long Christmas	$10.
00100023	289. Sing-a-Long Christmas Carols	$10.
00100073	290. "My Heart Will Go On" & 15 Other Top Movie Hits	$7.
00102124	293. Movie Classics	$9.
00100069	294. Old Fashioned Love Songs	$9.
00100303	295. Best of Michael Bublé	$12.
00100075	296. Best of Cole Porter	$7.
00102126	297. Best TV Themes	$7.
00102130	298. Beautiful Love Songs	$7.
00001102	301. Kid's Songfest	$9.
00102147	306. Irving Berlin Collection	$14.
00102182	308. Greatest American Songbook	$9.
00100194	309. 3-Chord Rock 'n' Roll	$8.
00001580	311. The Platters Anthology	$7.
02501515	312. Barbra – Love Is the Answer	$10.
00100196	314. Chicago	$8.
00100197	315. VH1's 100 Greatest Songs of Rock & Roll	$19.
00100080	322. Dixieland	$7.
00100277	325. Taylor Swift	$10.
00100082	327. Tonight at the Lounge	$7.
00100092	333. Great Gospel Favorites	$7.
00100278	338. The Best Hymns Ever	$19.
00100279	340. Anthology of Jazz Songs	$19.
00100280	341. Anthology of Rock Songs	$19.
00100281	342. Anthology of Broadway Songs	$19.
00100282	343. Anthology of Love Songs	$19.
00100283	344. Anthology of Latin Songs	$19.
00100284	345. Anthology of Movie Songs	$19.
00102235	346. Big Book of Christmas Songs	$14.
00100292	347. Anthology of Country Songs	$19.
00102140	350. Best of Billboard: 1955-1959	$19.
00100095	359. 100 Years of Song	$17.
00100096	360. More 100 Years of Song	$19.
00100103	375. Songs of Bacharach & David	$7.
00100107	392. Disney Favorites	$19.
00100108	393. Italian Favorites	$7.
00100111	394. Best Gospel Songs Ever	$17.
00100114	398. Disney's Princess Collections	$10.
00100115	400. Classical Masterpieces	$10.

HAL•LEONARD CORPORATION

7777 W. BLUEMOUND RD. P.O. BOX 13819 MILWAUKEE, WI 53213

Prices, contents, and availability subject to change without noti